Her Preaching Body

Her Preaching Body

Conversations about
Identity, Agency, and Embodiment
among Contemporary Female Preachers

AMY P. McCULLOUGH

CASCADE *Books* · Eugene, Oregon

HER PREACHING BODY
Conversations about Identity, Agency, and Embodiment among Contemporary
Female Preachers

Cascade Books
An Imprint of Wipf and Stock Publishers
199 W. 8th Ave., Suite 3
Eugene, OR 97401

www.wipfandstock.com

PAPERBACK ISBN: 978-1-4982-9163-7
HARDCOVER ISBN: 978-1-4982-9165-1
EBOOK ISBN: 978-1-4982-9164-4

Cataloguing-in-Publication data:

Names: McCullough, Amy P., author.
Title: Her preaching body : conversations about identity, agency, and embodiment
   among contemporary female preachers / Amy P. McCullough.
Description: Eugene, OR : Cascade Books, 2018 | Includes bibliographical references.
Identifiers: ISBN 978-1-4982-9163-7 (paperback) | ISBN 978-1-4982-9165-1 (hardcover) | ISBN 978-1-4982-9164-4 (ebook)
Subjects: LCSH: Preaching. | Women clergy. | Feminism—Religious aspects—Christianity.
Classification: BV4211.3 .M33 2018 (print) | BV4211.3 .M33 (ebook)

Manufactured in the U.S.A.   MAY 14, 2018

Dedication

This book is dedicated to the women of every generation who have boldly preached their faith.

Contents

Acknowledgments

It was the Apostle Paul who first offered the image of the church as a body, in which all the members of the whole play a vital role. I offer my gratitude for the following persons, with profound awareness this body of work would not have come to be without them. My husband, Chris, nurtured my dreams of studying homiletics from the very beginning, often at considerable costs to his own plans. His generous, steady spirit sustains our lives. Our children, Luke and Suzanna, teach me daily about embodiment. They also kept me on task by endlessly inquiring, "Is the book done yet?"

My interest in exploring the bodily decisions of female preachers began when I was a doctoral student in the Graduate School at Vanderbilt University. Professor Ted A. Smith contributed mightily to this work, offering not only his enthusiasm but also his sharp analytical insights and his talent for asking the right questions. Professors John S. McClure, Robin Jensen, and Ellen Armour each provided thoughtful feedback that deepened the scope of the research. Fellow students Katy Rigler, Noel Schoonmaker, Alex Tracy, Joshua Villines, and Rich Voelz formed a wonderfully rich and supportive community of scholars.

Several bodies of Christ have nurtured my faith, including the First United Methodist Church of Orlando, the Central Methodist Mission of Johannesburg, South Africa, and Metropolitan Memorial United Methodist Church of Washington, DC. I am grateful to Glenelg United Methodist Church for supporting this work while I served as their minister. And a special word of thanks to Grace United Methodist Church of Baltimore, Maryland, who generously blessed their pastor with time away to write, even during Advent. Kitty Allen offered her valuable proofreading skills when the book was in its final stages.

Other members of Christ's body offered spaces of hospitality at critical junctures in the research and writing of this book. Just as Paul asks where the body would be without the eyes or the ears, I know the enormous gift each one has given through their presence in my life: my parents, Fred and Nancy Peed, Mike and Andrea Peed, John and Kendra Allen, and George Stavros. Lastly, and most especially, I give thanks, with awe and sense of humility, for the women who so generously shared their stories of preaching, pastoring, and being women. The strength of their preaching embodiments will shine long after this book fades into the background. More than being grateful for their willingness to participate in the research, I am grateful that they are preachers. May this work honor them and the body of believers they serve.

Introduction: Questions about Bodies

When I was growing up, my family attended a large United Methodist church located in the downtown section of Orlando, Florida. The sanctuary was a broad, rectangular-shaped room, with high ceilings and a white marbled altar. The front stained glass windows stretched from ceiling to floor and created a second mosaic of colors across the white walls whenever the bright Florida sunshine poured through them. For a young girl sensing her call to ministry, it was a room of beauty, a hallowed space of silence, music, and, of course, sermons.

The preachers who strode up the stairs into the high pulpit stood in a long line of distinguished men, all of whom had received a plumb appointment and many of whom would go on to become bishops. Their preaching was solid if not soaring. I would try to listen, but often found myself watching the long arm of my father's watch get closer and closer—and sometimes even past—twelve noon. One Sunday, a visiting evangelist within the church growth movement of the 1980s preached the morning's message. For reasons now lost to memory, I attended all three of the morning worship services. By the time he started his last sermon, a message I suspect he had preached many times over, I had ceased listening to the words. Instead, I watched his body. He didn't move dramatically. Nor did he shout or scream. It appeared, though, that he was alive to his body. It was as if he had asked—and already answered—questions about whether a slight vocal inflection here might compel the listener to lean closer, whether this hand gesture there might drive home his words, and how to strike a balance between a posture fully posed and fully at ease. Fascinated by the interworking of his embodied speech, I wondered what he was experiencing

1

as the preacher. Is there a point when—for whatever reason—a preacher forgets about the words and thinks only about the body?

To think about the body as one preaches was a thought-provoking suggestion for Rev. Laura Martin. Experiencing a call to ministry in elementary school, she wondered how to present the profession to her family of bankers and scientists. "When I was around twelve," she recalled, "I was part of a youth program in the African Methodist Episcopal Church." She was invited to a church event with friends, learning later that she was expected to spend the night in order to attend worship the next morning. Not anticipating the overnight stay, Rev Martin had not packed any clothes. "The girls said, 'don't worry, we will let you wear our clothes,'" Rev. Martin continued. "I am five foot nine inches and they were five feet at that. So the jacket was short. The skirt was short. Everything was tight." When the next morning's preacher invited "young people who know they have been called by God" down to the altar at the end of his sermon, she remembered, "I sat in my chair and said, 'No way, God. Look at me. I'm not going up there.'" Rev. Martin concluded, "And God said 'Forget about you. I want your heart and your voice.' So I got up." On this occasion, Rev. Martin's entry into the preacher's life required a forgetting of her body, or at least of its clothed appearance. That forgetfulness would remain an integral part of her call to preach for years to come. If there are times to remember the body, are there other occasions that require letting go of it?

The dilemmas around remembering or forgetting the body, using or setting aside the body can weave their way through a preacher's narratives as she recognizes the link between her embodiment and her sermon. When I was a seminary student, the supervising minister at the church where I interned urged me to integrate an illustration about my deafness in one ear into an early sermon, insisting that the congregation needed to be informed about my hearing limitations. I disagreed with his opinion, but when faced with needing to pass my field education requirement I grudgingly complied. The sermon that arose out of those conversations stands as my most engaged and engaging sermon during divinity school. The body's inter-involvement in a sermon, as the instrument through which every preacher interprets life, text, and God may form a sermon in unanticipated or even unseen ways.

As the occasion of dilemmas and opportunities, the body brings a host of questions. Sometimes the questions are particular to one's physicality, such as those about a preacher's hearing loss or concerns about her height.

Sometimes the questions arise from cultural situated-ness, including the expectations of a denomination or a specific congregation. A preacher may debate about preaching in or out of the pulpit, as well as with or without notes. And sometimes the questions surrounding the body appear connected to gender. Female preachers know how devastating it can be to hear "What a pretty dress you have on!" at the end of a sermon long labored and lovingly performed. When preparing to officiate at a wedding, Rev. Rebecca Harris deliberately downplays her hairstyle, jewelry, and makeup. She said, "I don't want to show up the bride." During my doctoral coursework, I noticed the differences between my preaching as well as that of other female students and our male colleagues. These differences were not universal, and sometimes the variations were elements so slight I could not fully pinpoint them. Most notable were those occasions when I watched some male preachers utilize more gestures, vocal changes, and energetic styles. They appeared more physically at ease—and more physically active—than their female contemporaries. These observations raised questions about how the preacher engages bodily in preaching, as well as how preachers and listeners have come to conceive of a fully embodied sermon. How might gender inform and form the preacher's capacities for embodiment?

Throughout Christian history, the preaching body has most often been male. While women have been preaching since Mary ran from the empty tomb, the history of their preaching has been discontinuous, sometimes hidden, and filled with the struggle of bearing a female body in the pulpit.[1] For centuries church tradition argued the female body was unfit for sacred space. Cultural messages in other eras argued a woman's voice did not belong in the public sphere.[2] When women transgressed the boundaries to preach, they received criticism for behaving in unbecoming ways, provoking impure thoughts in male listeners, looking out of place in the pulpit, and having quieter, higher voices that could not be heard. While female preachers appear in almost every era of Christianity, it is only in the last three decades that women have occupied pulpits of well-established denominations in large numbers and with the full authority of ordination.

Just as many of the barriers female preachers historically encountered focused upon their bodies, the continuing dilemmas and decisions female

1. Brekus, *Strangers and Pilgrims*; Collier-Thomas, *Daughters of Thunder*; Kim, *Women Preaching*; Kienzie and Walker, *Women Preachers and Prophets*.

2. For illustrations of how female preachers navigated these cultural codes, see Florence, *Preaching as Testimony*, and Zink-Sawyer, *From Preachers to Suffragists*.

preachers face—concerning identity, authority, and the best use of their preaching skills—play out in their bodies. Women ask themselves questions about dress, wondering if a power suit will grant them authority or cause them to present an overly corporate appearance. They ponder the best way to preach in a small country church with a tiny pulpit that confines their body or, alternatively, in an exceptionally tall pulpit that requires a step stool in order to be seen. They question how to handle complaints that their voices cannot be heard while wondering about the hidden meanings within such feedback. Or they question what to do when the church's preaching schedule does not match the schedule of their breast-feeding baby and the cries of someone else's screaming infant cause their full breasts to leak. These questions are bodily ones. They are a preacher's questions.

My initial experiences and observations led me to ponder the physical inhibitions seeming to accompany female preachers. In her essay "Throwing Like a Girl," Iris Young names the ways in which girls grow up to be women who are physically handicapped, not employing completely their bodies' capabilities or inhabiting the world with the same degree of ease as their male counterparts.[3] She cites a study conducted during the 1960s by Erwin Straus in which girls did not make full use of lateral space in the act of throwing a ball. Concentrating on the forward movement of their arms, girls did not shift their weight, move their legs, or twist their hips. Young builds upon this study to argue that women "do not put their whole bodies into engagement in a physical task with the same ease and naturalness as men."[4] In surveying a very small slice of male and female preachers, I wondered if a female hesitancy, derived from a host of social messages and experiences, extends to the female in the pulpit. Young concludes that the bodily constraint felt by women broadens into a more general experience of space as constricted space.[5] As I thought about the female preaching students who stayed rooted in the pulpit alongside with the male students who easily left it, I wondered if women feel constrained while preaching. Perhaps the bodily uncertainty and timidity that Young first named twenty years ago still endures.[6]

The central problem underlining this initial bodily analysis is apparent to anyone who has studied the history of female preaching. For much of

3. Young, "Throwing like a Girl," 27–45.

4. Ibid., 33.

5. Ibid.

6. Ibid., 34.

Christian history, women were prohibited, discouraged, and heavily scrutinized for preaching.[7] For much of that same history, women preached. The history of women's persistence to preach, despite enormous institutional, social, theological, and even physical barriers, speaks not of hesitancy, uncertainty, and timidity but of boldness, courage, and risk. With arguments against their preaching citing their physical inferiority, female preachers endured constant attention, criticism, and outright ridicule directed toward their bodies. Countless women recorded long periods of bodily distress—noticed and surmounted—both when resisting a call to preach and when preaching.[8] To label female preachers as bodily inhibited does not account for these stories. An analysis of the female preacher's body based solely in notions of constraint fails to incorporate the multiple instances in which women preached in, with, and through their bodies despite intense pressure not to do so.

In her study of contemporary female preachers, Roxanne Mountford traces the gendered history of preaching manuals and the gendered construction of sacred spaces such that women's bodies were neither welcomed nor anticipated in pulpits. She studies three modern-day preachers in depth, arguing that two of them, feeling uneasy in the pulpit's proper space, made a tactical move to preach from the sanctuary floor. They decided to "quit the pulpit" in order to bring their preaching into the nave.[9] While Mountford's portrait of gendered space is invaluable, her very focused conclusion that women wrestle power from the pulpit to the floor stands in uneasy, inconclusive tension with other observations from women who preach both within and beyond the pulpit. When Rev. Shannon Baker arrived at her new church, she inherited a pulpit designed for her predecessor, a man well over six feet. "All they could see was my head," she remembered. But rather than abandon the pulpit, she worked with the congregation to reconfigure it to her size. She claims the pulpit, just as Rev. Joan Anderson does, who affirms, "I do stay behind the holy desk." In contrast to these preachers, Rev. Harris chooses to preach from the floor. Her decision rests not in "quitting the pulpit" but in getting closer to the listeners. She explained her preaching posture to her congregation in her first sermon. "The model of preaching that we get up in this tower and proclaim this word to you people down there . . . doesn't model the kind of pastor I want to be," she said. "There is

7. See, again, Brekus, *Strangers and Pilgrims*.

8. See Lawless, *God's Peculiar People*, and Lawless, *Holy Women*.

9. Mountford, *Gendered Pulpit*, 79–85.

something holy about preaching but in my embodied word theology, the word is not just embodied in me. It is in you. It is in all of us. So if I'm standing up here separate from you, it just doesn't work." So the choice to stay in the pulpit may arise from a female hesitancy in the body, a hesitancy made more pronounced in a setting in which all eyes are on the preacher. Or the choice may be a conscious decision to grasp the pulpit's authority, as a sacred site for preaching and the best place for conveying the message. The decision to preach outside the pulpit can be an equally empowering decision to embody a particular theology or make more effective use of the sanctuary space. Like most groups, female preachers across time, location, age, denomination, and experience will choose from a variety of bodily tactics when they preach. Their decisions are based on multiple factors, which can intersect and even compete. An analysis of the female preaching body needs not only to expand beyond a constraint-based argument; it also needs to possess enough porous flexibility to encompass ever-shifting factors and the ever-evolving, infinite uses of bodily power.

My experiences as a preacher and an observer of other preachers prompted a desire for further study. How does a larger field of female preachers think about and experience their bodies while they preach? Fourteen contemporary preachers weighed in on this question, reflecting on a host of decisions they made concerning their bodies as they prepared to and did preach.[10] Although a small selection, this eclectic group of preachers ranged in age from their mid-twenties to nearly seventy and came from diverse theological traditions. The majority of women were ordained United Methodist ministers, representing my own tradition. The group also represented the Presbyterian and Unitarian Universalist traditions. Joining these Christian ministers were two rabbis serving in Reformed Jewish congregations. The theological traditions of the study are limited to a particular brand of mainline Protestantism and a similar thread within Judaism. Neither "high" liturgical traditions like the Episcopal Church nor "low" liturgical traditions such as Pentecostalism were represented in the research. While other aspects of pastoral ministry did emerge during the interviews, the study maintained a focus upon the preacher in the pulpit or on the platform. The racial configuration of the group included African

10. The names of all interviewees are being held in confidence by mutual agreement. Each preacher was assigned a pseudonym. Direct quotations from interviews have been preserved, except in instances when details have been altered to maintain anonymity. Some identifying features of the preachers, their contexts, and their preaching habits also have been altered. For more detailed information about this study, see appendix A.

American and Caucasian women. Issues surrounding race and ethnicity were factored into the analysis, especially in those instances when the interviewee raised racial considerations. Such analysis is offered, though, with an acknowledgment that the depth and breadth needed for the fullest analysis may elude the scope of this project and the researcher, who is a white woman.

All of the participants recounted decisions about clothing, hair, and makeup when getting ready to preach and explained their approach to gestures, voices, and movements while preaching. Listening to their words and observing them as they preached, I was particularly interested in how they made decisions, the subsequent meaning they assigned to their choices, and how such meaning intersected with their body's behavior. In what ways did the body contribute to preaching? How was the body a powerful tool and when did it feel like a hindrance? Did the "femaleness" of their body, broadly construed as any trait associated with what is socially assigned to the feminine, play a prominent role in their decision- and meaning-making processes?[11] Arguing that we cannot understand any preacher without seeing her body nor fully account for her preaching without grasping the role the body plays in the performance, I contend that we cannot delve into the wide range of possible meanings attached to being a female and a preacher without paying close attention to the choices women make in relation to their bodies. In the process of making choices, women made meaning, in the making of meaning; women constructed their identity, and specifically their identity as preachers.

Questions of identity, agency, and meaning turn the focus to philosophy. The philosophical field of phenomenology begins with our basic experience of the world. It believes that meaning may be uncovered not as a thing in and of itself, but as that which flows out of and back into lived existence. In his seminal work *The Phenomenology of Perception*, Maurice Merleau-Ponty grounds perception, the basis of existence, in the body, naming the body as the mode through which we understand ourselves as "perceiving subjects in a perceived world."[12] The body is the vehicle for existence, or what he terms "being-in-the-world."[13] To have a body is "to

11. I employ the terms "masculine" and "feminine" to represent the traits, behaviors, and associations typically marked with the gender distinctions made between male and female bodies.

12. Merleau-Ponty, *Phenomenology of Perception*, 83.

13. Ibid., 90–93.

be intervolved in a definite environment, to identify with certain projects and be continually committed to them."[14] Trying to bridge the dichotomies entrenched in body and soul, subject and object; Merleau-Ponty describes the body as "always near me, always there for me, never really in front of me," but that which is with me.[15] The body is me or "rather I am it."[16]

Whenever one preaches, the preacher is her body. She senses her posture, notes her voice's pace, and gestures with her hands. We grasp our bodies, asserts Merleau-Ponty, by living in and with them. He writes, "I have no means of knowing the human body other than that of living it, which means taking up on my own account the drama which is being played out in it, and losing myself in it."[17] This body, he suggests, continually "rises towards the world."[18] As it is thrust into the world, the body becomes an ambiguous yet unified collection of lived experiences, and ultimately, "a nexus of living meanings."[19] When the preacher stands up to preach, she brings a collection of past experiences, memories of other uses of her body, and cultural messages about how to use the body. All of these are carried as present, vibrant meanings concerning her body. She might think, "Am I too short for this pulpit?" or "Can the congregation see my hands?" She might worry if listeners can hear her voice or sense her excitement. Whatever her "nexus of living meanings," they are distinct from the preacher before her and the preacher coming after her. Each preacher is a living body whose presence participates in proclamation and whose embodied decisions contribute to the meaning made from her message.

By being a collection of lived experiences, the body provides new insights into what it means to be a being in the world. The body does not possess knowledge separate from the mind. Rather, the mind is part of the body. By tracing all that inhabits the body, we move closer to a meaningful

14. Ibid., 94.

15. Ibid., 108.

16. Ibid., 173.

17. Merleau-Ponty states, "Whether it is a question of another's body or my own, I have no means of knowing the human body other than that of living it, which means taking up on my own account the drama which is being played out in it, and losing myself in it. I am my body, at least wholly to the extent that I possess experience, and yet at the same time, my body is as it were a 'natural' subject, a provisional sketch of my total being" (ibid., 230).

18. Ibid., 87.

19. Ibid., 170, 175.

core at the heart of existence.[20] Merleau-Ponty argues for relearning to feel our body, and finding "underneath the objective and detached knowledge of the body that other knowledge which we have of it by virtue of its always being with us and of the fact that we are our body."[21] These discoveries form the deeper knowing carried by the body as one moves about her world. Such discoveries are provisional ones; a partial glimpse into a total being that will never be fully apprehended.[22] But their provisional character does not render them less important. As Merleau-Ponty concludes, "We merge into this body which is better informed than we are about the world, and about the motives we have and the means at our disposal for synthesizing it."[23] We comprehend the world by living in it, we can only live in it as a body, and thus the body as a mode of inquiry provides essential clues into our world and ourselves.

What follows is an exploration of female preachers in their bodies. In one sense, it is another study about female preachers. It seeks to add to the collection of scholarship a new line of inquiry, balancing historical perspectives with contemporary experiences, complementing theological motifs with practical, ethnographic research. It asks, "What does it mean to be a body thrust into the world, a body that is a female and whose project is preaching?" From a different angle, this is a study concerned with how agency—the freedom and constraint that comes with choice—is worked out by those who have taken up a professional not long their own. Merleau-Ponty, among others, argues that the freedom to make choices happens because we are bound to embodied existence. Believing "there is no freedom without a field," he states, "This certain significance of nature and history which I am, does not limit my access to the world, but . . . is my means of entering into communication with it."[24] We can only choose because we have something to choose from, a particular setting and set of circumstances. We often define ourselves by the choices that we make and so any study of agency is by necessity a study of the evolving self. How do female preachers understand who they are, what they do, and why they do it? But ultimately, this is a study about bodies, or more precisely, embodied life. This is not a study about the body as opposed to the mind or the body

20. Ibid., 212.
21. Ibid., 239.
22. Ibid., 230.
23. Ibid., 277.
24. Ibid., 529.

as mere materiality. It risks the long association of the female with the body by delving into the bodily choices of female preachers. It looks at female preachers not because any one of us can be reduced to being "just a body" but because the contentiousness accompanying the female preaching body makes for a more accessible exploration. It argues that just as we are our bodies in every facet of life, we are our bodies when we preach. We preach in and through, with and as bodies, and thus every aspect of what we think about our bodies, every decision we ponder about our bodies, and every way we bring our bodies into the preaching space is bound up with the essence to be uncovered about preaching, even if that essence only can be partially uncovered.

Merleau-Ponty compares the body to a work of art.[25] Like every work of art, the body is a being "in which the expression is indistinguishable from the thing expressed, their meaning accessible only through direct contact."[26] Similar words can be uttered about preaching. Preaching is a work of art. And like every work of art, the sermon is the expression indistinguishable from the body preaching the sermon. Because "existence realizes itself in the body," to examine the body of the preacher is to explore the being of the preacher, the person in her entirety.[27] It is also to peer into preaching. Utilizing a small section of female preachers but delving deeply into their embodied preaching lives, this study will endeavor to achieve the same sort of aims Merleau-Ponty articulates for phenomenology: the painstaking work of essential exploration, which can only be done with attentiveness, wonder, and the will to size the meaning of the world, recognizing how that meaning is always coming into being.[28]

25. Ibid., 174.

26. Ibid., 175.

27. Merleau-Ponty writes, "If we therefore say that the body expresses existence at every moment, this is in the sense in which a word expresses thought. . . . In this way, the body expresses total existence, not because it is an external accompaniment to that existence, but because existence realizes itself in the body" (ibid., 193).

28. Ibid., xxiv.

CHAPTER 1

Living as a Body: Theories of Embodiment

The Reverend Rebecca Harris learned the hard way that it matters what shoes one wears to worship. Leading a Tenebrae service during Holy Week, she stepped across the chancel to extinguish a candle and the square, wooden heels of her black pumps clanked upon the slate floor. Within the dark, spacious, exceedingly quiet sanctuary the congregation experienced a reading from Jesus' passion, a full minute for silent reflection, and then the clop, clop, clop of her shoes as she walked from chair to altar. The sound reverberated across the space, disrupting the somber scene, and making Rev. Harris increasingly self-conscious about her body's necessary but distracting movements.

In her thirties, Rev. Harris was the first female and youngest preacher ever appointed to her United Methodist church. Charged with reviving a dwindling congregation, she inherited an enormous, once glorious, white-wooded sanctuary, complete with stained glass windows and an elevated pulpit reached by a tiny staircase. A college athlete who also had dabbled in drama, Rev. Harris approached her new church with a strong sense of her body and confidence in her preaching. She was accustomed to receiving positive responses to her sermons. She had preached long enough to experiment, preaching with and without a manuscript, as well as in and out of the pulpit. She had spent some months concentrating on word choice in her sermons and others emphasizing her body's movement. She once moved up and down a ladder while speaking. On another occasion, she illustrated the dance of the Holy Spirit by doing a grand jeté down the center aisle. Most Sundays, she made intentional, astute choices about how best to embody her preaching.

The ease with which Rev. Harris incorporated her body into her preaching did not mean that she disregarded her physical appearance. Wearing an alb most Sundays, she typically dressed in layers that afford her a business-casual appearance before and after worship while also insuring comfort beneath her alb during worship. Earrings stayed small so as not to interfere with her microphone headpiece. And notwithstanding her Holy Week experience, she chose her shoes carefully—not simply for noise potential—but also as the one piece of her appearance that might mark her femininity. "I want shoes that say I am a woman," she stated, "because I am a female preacher. I don't wear stiletto heels, of course, but I don't wear my Dansko clogs either." On one occasion when she led worship without an alb, she found her thoughts wandering to her appearance. Is this skirt too short? Is this sweater too low? Would someone else see these patterned tights as fishnet ones, as my husband did this morning? A proven, self-assured preacher, she did not escape the bodily concerns that confront most females in the pulpit. As she said, "I want to be fashionable, but not too fashionable. Who wants a fashion forward minister?"

All of these bodily considerations haunted her the Christmas Eve when she stood in the pulpit preaching about Christ's birth knowing that she had started to miscarry. Newly pregnant and having sensed something wasn't quite right from the beginning, Rev. Harris crafted images of babies, mangers, and God's coming in human flesh while her body shed a pregnancy. Suspended between incarnation and miscarriage, it was one of the few times that she shut out her body's messages, disconnecting the words of her sermon from the events within her own flesh.

The Body in Preaching

The body is central to preaching. Whether self-conscious about her clothing choices or empowered by a grand jeté, Rev. Harris always is in and with her body while she preaches. Her body is not one aspect of the proclamation but the vehicle of her task. Like every preacher before and after her, Rev. Harris's posture, dress, hairstyle, and facial expressions begin the sermon before she opens her mouth. Her decisions around the place from which to preach, whether to grip the pulpit or keep her hands by her side, how to inflect her voice, or what gestures to employ further enflesh the sermon. Some facets of the body are beyond choice, such as height or the shape of the hands. Others—like position, posture, and clothes—can be deliberate choices. Even others—like a miscarriage, illness, or the effects of aging—present themselves as life unfolds. These elements of embodiment work together to create a sermon. Since one cannot preach without her body, to explore preaching is to explore the body.

Rev. Harris's preaching embodiments offer some clues about the intersections between the body and preaching, between bodily life and embodied sermons. Her choice of shoes could distract a quiet congregation or signify her womanhood. Her athletic training gave her confidence to scale a ladder or dance down the aisle. She noticed the difference between preaching with and without an alb, aware that a lack of prescribed liturgical garments made her more susceptible to anxiety about her appearance. She articulated a theological link between her living self and her preaching, describing a sermon as a moment of embodying the Word. Presenting her particular embodiment, Rev. Harris illuminated the rich exploration possible in every preacher.

To explore Rev. Harris's preaching is to delve into a female body. Her notions of femininity as well as her capacity to conceive were woven into her experience of preaching. She emphasized her desire for shoes that conveyed her womanhood. At the same time, her shoe choices marked her boundaries for acceptability in the pulpit: no clogs and no stiletto heels. Another preacher will disagree with her, citing a similar focus on shoes to a different end. "I think the most about my shoe choice," said Rev. Baker, "because they are the one thing able to be seen beneath my alb. I always wear two inch, stiletto heels." Every embodiment is a particular embodiment, born of the specifics of one's physicality, culture, class, experience, and choices. A preacher brings her femaleness into the pulpit because she does not preach without the intricacies of her bodily life.

Any exploration of embodiment rests upon a theory of the body, a method of inquiry that offers a perspective about the interconnections of physicality and life. Considerable scholarship around the body has emerged in recent decades, recognizing how the body is integral to the self and a place from which individual, social, institutional, and political knowledge is revealed.[1] Feminist theory, while balancing competing truths about the body as a site of unique knowledge and the risks of reducing women solely to their bodies, has been integral to these developments. Such scholarship

---

1. Frank, "Bringing Bodies Back In," 131–62.

incorporates the distinction made between sex, as the biological characteristics accompanying male and female bodies, and gender, those roles, attributes, and behaviors assigned to masculinity and femininity within a culture. It holds the body as integral to understanding the dilemmas, burdens, choices, and potential contained within women's lives. As feminist theory has evolved, exactly how knowledge is gleaned through embodiment, as well as how women share and diverge in lived experiences, remains a topic for precise, honest exploration.

This chapter traces several theoretical approaches to the body. Essentialist theories argue that all women are connected through an irreducible, pure feminine essence, which originates in either shared biology or a set of common experiences. Social constructivist theories view essentialist positions as inadequate, both in describing the ways a body is formed and the plurality of bodily formations. They emphasize culture's vital role in crafting embodiments. Delving deeply into constructivist approaches with a notion of performativity, Judith Butler creates a bridge to a new theoretical approach. The lived body theory combines the insights of constructivist approaches, a renewed appreciation for the body's corporeality, and an emphasis on agency. Each of these approaches—and the dialogue prompted between them—continue to shape analyses of the female preacher's body. In the end, the lived body approach provides the strongest set of tools by which to explore female preachers' embodied decisions.

The Universal Female: Essentialist Approaches

As women began to preach in greater numbers during the last quarter of the twentieth century, a host of homiletical scholarship emerged devoted to female preaching. Some works unearthed an era of female preachers previously hidden. Other works traced the long struggle toward women's ordination, analyzing the theological, ecclesial, historical, and practical elements constitutive of those battles.[2] Still others shined a light upon an emerging set of qualities that appeared distinctive in female preaching.[3] All of this scholarship built upon a belief that there was something unique about being a female preacher. These forays into female preaching evidenced the

2. See Zink-Sawyer, *From Preachers to Suffragists*; Hudson, "Shall Women Preach"; Hogan, "Overthrow of the Monopoly"; Muir, *Petticoats in the Pulpit*.

3. Smith, *Weaving the Sermon*.

influence of the earliest strand of feminist thought, now understood as an essentialist approach to studying the female body.

Essentialism draws its name from its grounding in essences, those preexisting, inherent, and fixed qualities that make something what it is.[4] Working to reclaim and re-signify the female body, the feminist essentialist framework first exposes how the normative body is male. Scholars then describe the attributes particular to being female, touching upon a shared anatomy, shared experience of not being male, or shared characteristics associated with the feminine. The classic text, *Our Bodies, Ourselves*, revels in the female body and its subsequent shaping of the female self. Carol Gilligan's *In a Difference Voice* serves as landmark scholarship around core feminine traits, as she develops a moral scheme based on relational life and establishes a female ethic of care.[5] By focusing on those elements linking women to one another, this body of research moves toward the female in her most universal form, whether that form comes through anatomy, psyche, or approach to the world.[6] Scholars seek the core element that makes a woman a woman, regardless of history, geography, culture, or situation.

While homiletical scholarship has produced collections of female preachers' sermons or histories dedicated to female preachers, it has most fully reflected essentialism through attempts to enumerate a set of traits related to the feminine visible in women preachers. Carol Norén's *The Woman in the Pulpit* begins with the assertion that "the Sunday morning service is different when a woman preaches."[7] Drawing from her research, Norén proposes a set of behaviors female preachers frequently employ. She names the use of conditional clauses, exegetical frameworks that privilege the hidden, suppressed, or disadvantaged biblical characters, and self-disclosing illustrations. Norén is not alone in identifying unique gifts women bring to preaching. Other scholars celebrate inclusive styles of language, gender-based differences in communication, relational models of authority, and

4. Jones names essentialism as "any view of women's nature that makes universal claims about women based on characteristics considered to be an inherent part of being female" (*Feminist Theory*, 26); Fuss writes, "Essentialism is classically defined as a belief in true essences—that which is most irreducible, unchanging and therefore constitutive of a given person or thing" (*Essentially Speaking*, 2).

5. Gilligan, *In a Different Voice*.

6 Fuss notes how in feminist theory essentialism articulates itself through a belief in "a pure or original femininity, a female essence, outside of the social" (*Essentially Speaking*, 2).

7. Norén, *Woman in the Pulpit*, 9.

expanded definitions of preaching.[8] These scholars argue that it is different when a woman preaches—and different in certain reliable, predictable ways.

One gift of essentialism comes through the introduction of gender into the homiletical conversation. Essentialism affirms a woman's perception—and lived truth—that being female is crucial to who she is and how she preaches. It creates a platform for discussion about the ways women experience their collection of curves, breasts, hairstyles, voices, and ability to carry another life as factors in their proclamation. It acknowledges the challenges of being a female rather than male preacher, bringing light to the history of exclusion and suspicion that accompanies women into the pulpit. Another gift of the theory comes in its reclamation of the body as vital to one's lived experience. The assertion that "something is different when a woman preaches" names the truth that one's physicality participates in and shapes one's preaching.

Embedded within the essentialist approach lives the assumption that a female body and lived experiences link women to one another. Yet female bodies encompass all manner of shapes, sizes, heights, weights, skin colors, hair textures, and vocal ranges. Women are different than men but also diverge from one another by virtue of race, ethnicity, class, or geography. Asking women to identify primarily with a core, unchanging way of preaching "as a woman" can ask a preacher to discard the particularities of her bodily life and ignore other aspects of lived experience that provide wisdom and shape preaching practices.

The crux of essentialism lies in the assertion that women are different from men in shared and consistent ways.[9] Even as they affirm its retrieval efforts, scholars criticize the theory's minimization of the diversity of women's bodies and lives. For every slight, short, soft-spoken woman there is a tall, deep-throated one. For every woman who gravitates to frilly blouses and pink suits, there is a woman who dons buttoned-down shirts and black slacks. Communal expectations for what it means to be female and for how to best present the female body differ widely across culture, time, and even Christian theology. To name women as different from men

8. See Ziel, "Mother Tongue"; Hartman, "Feminist Norms in Preaching"; Tisdale, "Women's Ways of Communicating," 104–16; Kim, "Conversational Learning," 169–77. The feminist theorists undergirding this scholarship include Gilligan; Tannen, *You Just Don't Understand*; Belenky et al., *Women's Ways of Knowing*.

9. Jones, *Feminist Theory*, 24.

is all too often to halt prematurely a discernment of difference, never delving beneath the first binary distinction to analyze the complexity existing among all women.

Essentialist approaches further stumble in naively hoping that the process of uncovering a female essence might eradicate gender hierarchy. The reality is that any notion of a pure femininity, in fact, may simply reproduce the stratification.[10] To call female preaching uniquely female is to set it apart from male preaching, which has not lost its normative, privileged status. To say that female preachers may inhabit their bodies in ways divergent from those normally described in preaching manuals does not dismantle the authority obtained via centuries of homiletical performance and literature. Nor does it affect the expectations, histories, or theologies of the congregation in which one might preach. Just as a belief in the universal woman gives way to an appreciation for the diverse contexts of women's lives, a belief in the power of naming female difference gives way to a need for further analysis of culture's role in how bodies are formed, perceived, and experienced. Essentialism begins the conversation about the possible meanings accompanying the female preacher. It marks the female body as one carrying a set of dilemmas, questions, and possibilities linked to its femaleness. Ultimately, though, those very questions necessitate more complex responses.

The Body Not Given but Formed: Constructivist Approaches

Cultural constructivist theories respond to the stumbling blocks named in essentialist frameworks with an analytical turn toward culture's profound influence on the body's formation. Rather than proposing that our bodies are the product of the passive outworking of an internal essence, these theorists assert that the body is molded over time in relationship to the social forces in which it is inevitably located.[11] Rather than emphasizing women's universal commonalities and shared experience, this approach unpacks the impact of context, community, tradition, race, and history on embodiment. It demonstrates how diverse bodies come to be and how variations happen in a body's presentation and reception. These forays into

10. Ibid., 29–30.

11. Jones writes, "Feminist constructivism can be defined as a theory that focuses on the social, cultural, and linguistic sources of our views of women and women's nature" (ibid., 32).

bodily construction create space for the critical analysis of culture's role in structures of gender hierarchy.

Drawing upon Simone de Beauvior's statement "women are made not born," constructivist approaches affirm that life is inextricably social and bodies are inescapably socialized.[12] Every body comes into being amid a culture, whose values, customs, history, and habits shape the body's development.[13] These contingent and variable social forces play a primary role in assigning meaning to body types, presentations, and behaviors. Certain bodies in certain cultures are affirmed as stronger, more attractive, or more believable. Certain behaviors, styles of dress, or manners of interacting are deemed acceptable, while others are labeled unacceptable. Since bodies can never lie outside of culture, ideas surrounding a woman's inherent qualities now are understood as reflections of a particular society's images and expectations of femininity. Thus, "bodies are not only physical phenomena, but also surfaces of inscription, loci of control and transmitters of culture."[14]

As surfaces of inscription, bodies bear the marks of culture. One strand of constructivist theories focuses upon the ways in which culture becomes written upon bodies.[15] Viewing the body as chock full of clues, these scholars encourage the understanding of the female preacher's body as a cultural text. Within contemporary American culture, women's bodies receive and reflect expectations about physical beauty, professionally appropriate personas, pregnancy, motherhood, and more. Mass media's onslaught of images conveys these messages, presenting through multiple channels the perfect body, whether it is working, working out, or bearing a child. Female preachers are not immune to such intense idealized images of femininity or the links between a symbol, style, or color and a gender-coded message. Rev. Harris's exclusion of clogs from the pulpit hinted toward a less-than-acceptable brand of femininity for her, at least for preaching. Another preacher will narrate an episode when her shoe color created a stir within her congregation as a signifier of promiscuity. Historically women have borne the connections made between physical beauty and moral character, many of which are racially coded. Nineteenth-century white

12. Ibid.

13. Drawing upon the work of Kathryn Tanner, Jones defines culture as "the entire system of symbols, languages, beliefs, actions, and attitudes within which persons live and learn to organize and make sense of their world and actions" (ibid., 33).

14. Lindman and Tarter, *Centre of Wonders*, 2.

15. Bordo, *Unbearable Weight*, 165.

female preachers often matched their bodily presentations with prevailing images of virtuosity in order to establish their preaching authority. Lastly, female preachers enter a professional context as well as a theological one. They may find themselves conforming to expectations for business suits or more formal Sunday attire. Or they may find themselves gravitating toward a subdued appearance that includes hair drawn away from the face and minimal jewelry, effectively neutralizing their gender. As a cultural text, the female preaching body and the reactions it receives provide a lens through which to grasp the multilayered and multiple worlds the preacher inhabits.

Some constructivist theories go beyond viewing the body as a site of inscription to argue that culture shapes the body in its materiality, at the level of the flesh. By crafting meaning-making structures, models of behavior, and patterns of interpersonal interaction, culture is literally "made body."[16] Culture determines what the body can or cannot do, makes possible certain bodies and renders other bodies impossible.[17] Historically, culture was "made body" in preaching through a tradition that asserted only men could preach. Relying upon societal messages linking women with the body in its most base, brute, and unthinking form while assigning men the higher category of rational thought, the female was deemed unfit to preach. The present-day preachers of this study inherited those centuries of exclusion, which often manifested through intense scrutiny of their embodiments. One preacher narrated a congregation's encouragement to trim down her size. Women who were nursing infants spoke about their self-consciousness concerning breast size, as well as the congregation's attention to their now shrinking bodies. Such analyses respond to essentialist arguments about an autonomous female voice with assertions about the role of culture in denying or limiting the social space in which a female could speak.

The social constructivist framework emphasizes that any study of embodiment must account for the intimate linkage between a particular body and its larger location. It asks scholars to explore the ways bodies are always embedded within a network of formal and informal relationships, to acknowledge the diversity of bodies made possible by differing communal contexts, and to examine the multiple ways in which culture manifests on the body. What might have appeared as a natural fact of existence is

16. Ibid.

17. Grosz indicates that this stance asserts that historical, social, and cultural factors "actively produce the body as a body of a determinate type" (*Volatile Bodies*, x).

revealed as a cultural construct by this set of theorists, who perceive of the body as constantly being formed amid interactions with other bodies and a vast, varying social network.[18]

Cultural constructivist approaches, though, encounter several stumbling blocks. As theorists grow more and more sophisticated in analyzing culture's impact upon the body, the sphere of that influence is cast wider and wider. Theorists risk veering into cultural determinism, in which the body is entirely formed by external forces beyond her control, neglecting an individual's agential power.[19] Bodies do not always conform to cultural structures, any more than they conform to essentialist ideals. Furthermore, women report, and seem to display, some experience of agency in bodily decisions. Lastly, cultural constructivists acknowledge that their theoretical work has moved far away from actual bodies.[20] As ever-expanding theories become increasingly abstract, scholars name the need to balance the theory with accounts of the body in its messy, material existence.

These issues limit constructivist insights into the female preaching body. Female preachers, like women in other spheres of society, have historically demonstrated tremendous transgressions to social expectations. Some women who felt called to preach entered sacred spaces that officially barred their presence. Some women violated communally acceptable ways of being female through their dress and behavior. Contemporary preachers continue to display a wide range of relationships to prevailing standards of idealized femininity, demonstrating both how culture is inscribed on bodies and how bodies can resist culture. Culture does influence the body's form, performance, and reception, but it is by no means the only factor affecting the female preaching body. A tradition born in the breaking of social and theological sanctions may not be best illuminated by a theory that explores bodily life through this single lens.

18. Griffith writes, "As countless scholars influenced by feminist, postcolonial, and other subaltern theories have long noted, bodies are not 'natural' in any simple sense but are made, through extensive cultural work, to seem that way: that is, they are 'naturalized'" (*Born Again Bodies*, 7).

19. Birke, *Feminism and the Biological Body*, 34. See also Jones, *Feminist Theory*, 41.

20. Fortunati et al., *Controversial Women's Body*, 76. Also, Birke attributes the recent focus on Foucault and the social forces that discipline the body for the ways within theoretical scholarship that "the body disappears as a material entity" (*Feminism*, 137).

The Performing Body: Judith Butler

One constructionist scholar, Judith Butler, addresses the weaknesses within constructionist approaches by proposing a theory of performativity. Focusing on gender formation, Butler argues that embodied selves are formed by the acts they commit. She traces how "the stylized repetition of acts through time" come to appear natural even as they originate in social structures with organized expectations for male and female bodies.[21] She writes, "bodily habitus constitutes a tacit form of performativity, a citational chain lived and believed at the level of the body."[22] While specific in its focus on gender identity, Butler's work introduces a new language, the language of performance.

Performance, as those acts repeated so continuously as to become unconscious enactments, orients scholars toward a close reading of specific embodiments. It invites an exploration of a body's behaviors, habits, and features, asserting that those behaviors, habits, and features have been acquired over time and at the intersection of culture's influence and repetitive actions. Using Butler's insights, scholars study how certain embodiments become solidified for a female preacher, with an appreciation for the formational role of cultural messages, as well as for how actions taken in response to social or gender expectations reinforce themselves. The same performative process can be applied to the cultural and theological structures assigned to preaching. Potential directives such as "the confident preacher ascends to the pulpit" and "the effective voice varies its sound" are congealed when preachers repeatedly choose the pulpit or modulate their voices. Preachers are shaped by their reoccurring choices.

Butler's evocative phrase defining performance as "stylizations of the body" illuminates this process.[23] Every preacher exhibits a variety of bodily habits, from the squaring of the shoulders to the clearing of the throat, from the flip of the hair to the grasping of the pulpit. Some preachers firmly plant themselves with feet shoulder width apart. Others twist an ankle behind one foot. Others preach barefoot. These fleshly stylizations perform a sermon. Just as preachers rely upon reoccurring theological motifs, preachers exhibit habits within their embodiments. Preaching itself is a repetition of actions, a stylization of the flesh that acquires its own cultural and

21. Butler, *Gender Trouble*, 192.

22. Butler, *Excitable Speech*, 115.

23. Butler, *Gender Trouble*, 191.

theological message. Studying these stylizations of the flesh aids in understanding female preachers.

Although bodies perform out of the structures that produce them, Butler acknowledges there will be unauthorized uses of bodily performances.[24] Embodied selves will tailor more generalized movements to suit their own particularity or will violate cultural expectations to perform actions in unsanctioned ways. With this acknowledgment Butler moves beyond any strict sense of cultural determinism to include individual agency in a theory of the body. Her schema of authorized and unauthorized performances mirrors the reality of earlier female preachers, whose bodies enacted unapproved performances amid systems that forbade their presence. With time, these violating performances created space for newly authorized behaviors, and eventually for new cultural structures. Women's exhortations in their home parlors, over centuries, transformed into institutionally legitimated female preachers in the pulpit or on the stage. Contemporary female preachers, in turn, experiment with various embodiments of femininity through everything from clothing choices to word selections to intonations of the voice. These performances create new shifts in the established parameters around preaching bodies.

Butler contributes mightily to the study of the body. Her influence includes her clearer articulation of the relationship between agency and embodiment as well as her recognition of the "insistent reality of bodies" as the site at which individuals perform.[25] Her argument that our bodies perform and by performing are formed into a self remains key to any understanding of embodiment. Focusing upon the body's ongoing performance, she also introduces a sense of the body's incompleteness. Bodily life is constantly shifting, always moving in relationship to itself and other bodies, always under development, and thus always moving toward but not attaining completeness.[26]

While Butler is most often characterized as a pure cultural constructivist, the complexity of her work does not lend to easy classification.[27] Her theory of performativity has generated much subsequent scholarship and

24. Kirby writes that, for Butler, identity and agency do not dissolve "when they are regarded as the embedding effects of cultural forces" (*Judith Butler*, 44).

25. Ibid., 66.

26. Butler, *Gender Trouble*, 33–34.

27. I would argue that Butler acknowledges the importance of flesh, but tends toward the power of language to constitute the self. She lifts up the power of agential choice, but by and large the performative acts she describes are culturally inscribed ones.

a new attention to agency and corporeality. At the same time, Butler can share the constructionist tendency toward abstraction from the very material realities to which she would call our attention. Often focusing upon the power of language, her scholarship veers away from a close reading of actual, particular bodies, even while naming the body as something that "exceeds the speech it occasions."[28] Nevertheless, the depth of her inquiry highlights the growing edges within studying embodied life. In this sense, she serves as a key transitional scholar who helps give birth to a new approach to studying the body. Building from her insights, and drawing upon the work of essentialist and other constructivist theories, a third framework for studying the body emerges. This approach seeks to integrate the continual influence of culture, the role of agency, and the specifics of the flesh together as mutually interacting elements of bodily life.

My Body as It Is Lived by Me: Lived Body Approaches

While essentialist approaches help bring the female body back into focus, they stumble in their strong emphasis upon female commonalities. While constructivist approaches offer an appreciation for culture's influence upon the body's formation, they are weakened by a sense of cultural determinacy that named the social as the main arbitrator of what a body can do or be. Butler's notion of performativity adds a layer of material analysis, yet it stumbles with an emphasis on linguisticality over flesh. Examining the strengths and weaknesses of each approach, three factors emerge as integral to any study of embodiment: a body's specific physicality, its cultural situation, and its exercise of agency. A final theory, the lived body approach, combines these elements into a framework that explores the embodied, experiencing person grounded in everyday life.

The lived body approach, also known as "the communicative body" or "the body in situation," builds on the insights of phenomenology to explore how individuals experience in and through their bodies a life that is inescapably social and inextricably material.[29] This approach views physicality, cultural influence, and individual choice as three interwoven, constantly

28 Butler, *Excitable Speech*, 155–56. In a way that illuminates the gap between Butler's more constructionist position with a lived body one, Butler devotes significant attention to linguistification. She argues that there is no natural foundation of the body that precedes language, and by extension, culture.

29. Weiss, *Intertwinings*, 1.

interacting, and shifting aspects of the self. It argues for the study of bodies in their specificity over "the body" as any universal, uniform thing.[30] Seeking to stay as close as possible to the body's materiality, lived body theorists argue that bodies are inherently diverse and constantly changing in choices and formations across time. By acknowledging the multiple factors involved in embodiment and attending to how life plays out in the flesh, the lived body approach provides the necessary tools for studying female preachers. It offers a framework for analyzing the physicality of preaching, the weight of religious and social messages about female bodies, and the multiple decisions women face while preaching.

Philosophical Foundations: Maurice Merleau-Ponty

The philosophical foundations supporting a lived body approach emerged from the scholarship of Frenchman Maurice Merleau-Ponty.[31] Working through a phenomenological account of perception, Merleau-Ponty diverged from the prevailing philosophical wisdom of his time to assert that the body, and not the mind, was the ground of all existence and the foundation of perception.[32] He states, "I am conscious of the world through the medium of my body."[33] Rather than perception originating with cognition, perception begins with the body's lived experience in the world. Merleau-Ponty categorizes such lived experience as the body's *motility*, or its experience of being "thrown into the world." Out of motility, the body realizes its subjectivity as a "being-in-the-world."[34] All subsequent perceptions—about one's physicality and surrounding reality—are constituted by the concrete structures and capacities of the body, as it inhabits the world into which it has been thrust. Thus, the body is the condition and context through which a person relates.[35]

30. Grosz, *Volatile Bodies*, 19.

31. For two surveys of Merleau-Ponty's contributions to the lived body theory, see Grosz, *Volatile Bodies*; Reynolds, *Merleau-Ponty*.

32. Merleau-Ponty, *Phenomenology of Perception*, 94–95.

33. Ibid., 94.

34. Ibid., 90.

35. Grosz, *Volatile Bodies*, 86. Merleau-Ponty also emphasizes how knowledge is bodily. He writes, "This knowledge, like other knowledge, is acquired only through our relations with other people" (*Phenomenology of Perception*, 110).

Having named the body's centrality, Merleau-Ponty further explores how coherence is created through embodied life. He asserts that an exploration of lived experience provides a window into the body's "meaningful core," a relatively stable set of actions and meanings attached to those actions built through our location in a specific material and inter-human world.[36] Bodies develop complex body schema, a series of fields relating to possible actions or movements in which the body "knows" how to perform and that simultaneously structure the body.[37] Defined as "a compendium of our bodily experience," the body schema creates a unified world in which the embodied self operates in practical relationship with other objects and with some degree of awareness of its embodied motions.[38] Through these various corporeal schemata a person gains a working knowledge of how to relate in the world. Reality becomes lived reality, derived from the body's unfolding involvement in its larger environment.

Merleau-Ponty provides three insights that form the foundations for the lived body theory. First, he conceives of experience, while privileged in consciousness, as always embodied. Reflections about living are grounded in our physicality. He states that "existence realizes itself in the body."[39] It is "a perpetual incarnation."[40] Our bodies experience the world. Our minds participate in and process those experiences and these body and mind interactions occur in tandem with each other. This perspective directly challenges any sense of pure consciousness or an essentialist notion that bodies arrive with an inherent, ahistorical sense of being. Next, embodied living amid a coherent corporeal schema results in the acquisition of bodily habitations. Here, the body's repetitive tasks leave "traces" upon the body, such that a body knows how to act in certain familiar situations, in the same way one's body can retain the knowledge of riding a bike.[41] Similar to Butler's stylizations of the flesh, Merleau-Ponty provides a description of how bodies acquire enfleshed proficiencies. And finally, the processes involved in

36. Merleau-Ponty, *Phenomenology of Perception*, 170. This meaningful core is a union of essence and existence, with essence comprised of a network biological and physiological functions and existence pertaining to the always-social experience.

37. Ibid., 113–15. He writes, "Those actions in which I habitually engage incorporate their instruments into themselves and make them play a part in the original structure of my own body" (104).

38. Ibid.

39. Ibid., 192.

40. Ibid.

41. Grimshaw, "Working Out with Merleau-Ponty," 112.

habitations solidify the embodied subject's movement toward meaning.[42] Merleau-Ponty locates meaning as arising amid the embodied subject's interactions with other objects, including other embodied subjects. We are not born with preset meanings attached to our bodies nor do the meanings developed about our existence derive solely from a culture's already established structure of meaning. Meaning is made in the individual's encounter with its situations.[43]

Merleau-Ponty's account of bodily existence deepens the reflective work possible within preaching. Preaching rests upon the embodied self, becoming one manifestation of a unified body and mind that seeks meaning as a being in the world. Furthermore, his insights around how an embodied person learns to perform are applicable to the manner in which the messages preachers receive around stance, posture, and voice settle into their bodies. These habitations, which are key to any person's functioning sense of self, are also critical in proclamation, even if the preacher cannot fully articulate how she acquired expertise in cadence, rhythm, or gestures. Merleau-Ponty's careful delineation of the learning process occurring in and through embodiment is especially key for female preachers, who navigate complex and conflicting corporeal schemata concerning how, when, and to what effect their preaching bodies can perform.

Embodiment as Physicality, Culture, and Choice

The lived body theory grows out of Merleau-Ponty's philosophical assertions. The term draws from his definitions of the body as "my-body-as-it-is-lived-by-me" or the body as "being-to-the-world."[44] Building upon his assertions, subsequent theorists explore bodies as they are experienced, analyzing the multiple meaning-making processes that happen as complex and ever-acting bodies are launched into the world filled with other complex and ever-acting bodies.[45] Remaining true to Merleau-Ponty's foundational

---

42. Merleau-Ponty writes, "To learn to see colors is to acquire a certain style of seeing, a new use of one's own body: it is to enrich and recast the body schema. Whether a system of motor or perceptual powers, our body is not an object for an 'I think,' it is an grouping of lived-through meanings which moves toward its equilibrium" (*Phenomenology of Perception*, 177).

43. Busch, "Existentialism," 32–33.

44. Grosz, *Volatile Bodies*, 86.

45. Merleau-Ponty, *Phenomenology of Perception*, 193.

thoughts, lived body approaches view embodied life as a constant becoming born of three intersecting threads. An individual's particular physicality, specific cultural context, and unique exercise of agency interact together to shape the self. Each piece of the body's puzzle is equally important. Scholars strive to remain close to the flesh and to notice the manifestations of culture and agency playing out across the embodied, experiencing individual.

Mirroring the body's diverse process of becoming, these scholars offer several different definitions of the lived body approach. Tamsin Wilton conceives of the body as "an event" continuously coming to be amid the back and forth of the material and the social.[46] Elizabeth Grosz imagines the body as a Mobius strip, in which mind and body continually bend back into each other.[47] This model, deeply influenced by Merleau-Ponty, enables the body to be understood as "open materiality," a fleshy presence within which certain tendencies and potentials emerge out of the interacting factors of physicality, society, and agency.[48] Young names the lived body theory as "a unified idea of a physical body acting and experiencing in a specific sociocultural context; it is the body-in-situation."[49] Although shaped by physicality and sociocultural context, the embodied self dwells in her situation, a space unique to that one body as a product of the individual's facticity and freedom. Facticity describes "the material facts of a person's body and its relation to a given environment," including physical attributes, skills, tendencies, and the larger givens of one's social environment.[50] Such facts of the body evolve in relationship to the body's freedom, as one chooses how to respond to those physical, social, and interpersonal realities of their daily life.[51]

A female preacher experiences herself as a body in situation. She navigates the facts of her physicality as her preaching style is shaped by her height, weight, vocal capacities, and perceptions of feminine beauty. She is shaped by the social factors of her congregation, tradition, and larger culture. She makes decisions in relation to those facts. Some decisions

46. Wilson conceives of the body as "an event situated in time and continuously subject to the con-constitutive dialectic of the organic and the social" ("Temporality," 59).

47. Grosz describes the Mobius strip as "the inverted three-dimensional figure eight," which twists, turns, and inverts such that one side becomes another (*Volatile Bodies*, xii).

48. Ibid., 191.

49. Young, "Lived Body versus Gender," 16. See also Moi, "What Is a Woman?"

50. Young, "Lived Body versus Gender," 16.

51. Ibid., 18.

are conscious ones born from an awareness of her given situation. Some choices are more reflexive. Her particular choices may or may not correspond to another preacher's choices when faced with a similar set of facts. One female preacher may utilize a step stool in order make more of her physical body visible from behind the pulpit. Another preacher, similar in height, may step outside the pulpit and preach from the sanctuary floor. One preacher may respond to her conceptions of being female by donning explicit cultural markers of femininity, whether it is makeup, jewelry, a dramatic hairstyle, or high-heeled shoes. Another may choose to downplay any cultural feminine markers and put on a white alb. While some decisions may be consciously considered before preaching, many of these choices appear to happen without forethought. Insight emerges as a person reflects upon the links between her body, culture, and actions, even as a full understanding of her agency will prove elusive.

Every female preacher encounters the fact that she engages in a practice that, for much of Christian history, was reserved for male bodies. And while few female preachers would choose to step into a space in which their bodies receive scrutiny, suspicion, and inhospitality, the ways in which women respond to these unchosen facts are endless. Delving into the complexity behind these choices, the lived body approach provides a workable set of tools to study the multilayered diversity of female preaching embodiment. In this study, the lived body approach will allow the researcher to look at these female preachers as utterly unique individuals, while recognizing the relationship of their choices to cultural messages about masculinity and femininity as well as with theological discussions about preaching. The women's choices also are formed within their physicality. Thus the study aims to stay very close to actual bodies propelled into specific contexts, believing that meaning is uncovered by observing female preachers as "beings-in-the-world." In so doing, it enables the theoretical dimension often missing from body conversations: a space to speak in practical turns about constraint and freedom, boundaries and breeches, meaning making and mystery.

Particularities of the Flesh: Habitation and Agency

The lived body theory has developed from its philosophical roots in Merleau-Ponty's work. Within this study of female preachers, however, his contributions around embodied habitations prove particularly helpful.

Habitations are those acquired traits operating in the body that hint at culture, physicality, and individual practice but often remain hidden from conscious comprehension. Habitations can illuminate the intricate avenues through which an individual makes choices about her body, which then leads to a discussion of agency. Agency is the moment of choice when an individual moves toward a particular action. Agency highlights how a person navigates her facticity and freedom, while acknowledging the complexity involved in all behaviors. Much mystery remains around how a person arrives at her unique expression of the self, even as habitations and agency widen the avenues of exploration.

Fleshy Habitations: What the Body Knows

Merleau-Ponty argues that bodily traces, those imprints in the body of its own motility, become, through time and repetition, ingrained practices. Having acquired a set of skilled movements, the body can act with a working, informed proficiency in its own given context. Habitations are fleshly proficiencies through which the body evidences its relational capacity in the world.[52] Through habitations, an embodied self comes to possess a world and then endows that world with significance.[53]

Merleau-Ponty utilizes habitations within his overarching quest toward essences, which he understands not as unchanging givens but as "cores of primary meanings."[54] In this sense, he names the way in which the body acquires knowledge. A habit is not a given. A habit is learned, signifying that the body learns through its own actions and carries that knowledge at the level of the flesh. This fleshly knowledge becomes "what the body knows," a phrase signifying the insight, wisdom, or truth an embodied life carries, which may or may not be fully accessible through verbal speech. Those who study the body have argued consistently that there is knowledge

52. Merleau-Ponty, *Phenomenology of Perception*, 162–65.

53. Merleau-Ponty writes, "The body is our general medium for having a world. Sometimes it is restricted to the actions necessary for the conservation of life, and accordingly it posits around us a biological world; at other times, elaborating upon these primary actions and moving from their literal to a figurative meaning, it manifests through them a core of new significance: this is true of motor habits such as dancing. Habit is merely a form of this fundamental power. We say that the body has understood and habit has been cultivated when it has absorbed a new meaning, and assimilated a fresh core of significance" (ibid., 169).

54. Ibid., xvii–xviii.

held in the body. Discerning "what the body knows" and how the body acquires such privileged knowledge remains a key element of any study of the body.[55]

In a corresponding manner, habitations are significant in understanding the ways in which preachers come to know in their bodies how they preach. Preaching involves habituating actions, as traces of the body's preaching experiences are refined through time and repetition into solid, continuous, and familiar behaviors. Preachers also bring into the pulpit an import of other habitations; those learned bodily acts arising from a preacher's history, physicality, context, and choices. Preaching informs the flesh, the flesh informs its own preaching, and through a long process of practice the body gains its preaching style.

Each female preaching body has its habitations and through them, holds knowledge. That knowledge may emerge in vague discomfort at standing in a space long denied to one's particular embodiment. It may surface through juggling social rules concerning diet, makeup, and dress as well as the complicated legacy of Christian distinctions between body and spirit. Insight can come through the experience of preaching good news in a stylization that is welcomed, gestures that work, or a voice that reaches the rafters and knows it is being heard. What the body knows weaves itself into the preacher's proclamation, becoming integral to how the flesh speaks. By exploring the preacher's habitations, the scholar can delve into the rich pool of wisdom brought by embodiment and move closer to what the body knows beyond speech.[56]

55 Turner asserts, "Bodies provide a different set of knowledge. We know with our bodies, and if there is any truth, it is the truth of the body" (*Body and Society*, 4). Early feminist theorists spoke at length about "women's ways of knowing," which often connected to their bodies. See Belenky et al., *Women's Ways of Knowing*. The same assertion is made from a different perspective by Frank, *Wounded Storyteller*. What remains contested is what exactly the body knows. Essentialist ideas center upon women's shared knowledge. Constructionist approaches point to the ways in which a woman's body will know a culture's representation of the female. A lived body perspective leaves open any firm conclusions about what the body might know, suggesting that specific, particular knowledge emerges in the fleshly tasks of everyday life.

56. Judith Butler remains firm that the gap between body and speech is healed through language. She suggests that as one tries to speak about that which is in excess of speech, one "renders discursive what is extra or nondiscursive" (*Excitable Speech*, 184). Other theorists name the limits of Butler's reliance upon a system of signification. Mahmood asks, "How do we develop a vocabulary for thinking conceptually about forms of corporeality that, while efficacious in behavior, do not lend themselves easily to representation, elucidation, and a logic of signs and symbols?" and suggests a "theory of

How a Body Chooses: The Intricacies of Agency

The habitations of the flesh and the knowledge they provide influence another vital element of any study of embodied life: the individual's exercise of her agency. Agency, as the potential for action, empowerment, and choice, appears, in varying degrees, within all body theories. By making agency one of its three main components, the lived body theory provides a window into the complexity contained within the choices we make. Agency emerges at the intersection of physicality and culture, at the point of contact between an individual life and larger tradition, between facticity and freedom. Agency illustrates how our choices can be far more bound than we can imagine while also possessing far greater possibility than we can foresee. Recognizing that embodied life is inherently social, Butler argues that agency emerges when a person chooses to endorse a system of meaning that exerts influence upon her as well as when she resists against it.[57] Like habitations, the choices made by an embodied self are not easily grasped in all their fullness.

The process of exploring agency requires an analysis of the factors influencing a particular choice, the process by which a person makes the decision, and the impact resulting from the subsequent choice. Just as the staying power of a habitation evolves over time, the choices we have made shape the choices we will make and what it feels like to live as a body within the boundaries of our choices over time. Agency happens in the body. Thus, exploring the how, why, and to what effect accompanying every choice moves the scholar closer to Merleau-Ponty's core of meaning within embodied existence.[58] Such a core of meaning can never be reduced to simple cause and effect dynamics, nor is it ever completely uncovered.

---

linguistic signification does not quite apprehend the power that corporeality commands" (*Agency*, 203).

57. Butler's main thesis is that the subject comes into being when the forces which first exerted external control upon a person are assumed internally, giving birth to the psyche itself. She asks, "What does it mean, then, that the subject, defended by some as a presupposition of agency, is also understood to be an effect of subjection?" (*Psychic Life of Power*, 11).

58. Merleau-Ponty is very clear that this "meaningful core" holds deep knowledge without being a universalizing truth. He writes, "To see the essence of perception is to declare that perception is, not presumed true, but defined as access to truth. The world is not what I think, but what I live through. I am open to the world, I have not doubt that I am in communication with it, but I do not possess it; it is inexhaustible" (*Phenomenology of Perception*, xviii–xix).

Even when it appears the self chooses in freedom, a set of confinements work to restrict the choice.[59] Such confinements establish the possibility of choice, even as they are altered by the decisions the self embraces. Furthermore, the choices that we make can surprise us, illuminating the elusive ambiguity that is part and parcel of embodied life. To explore agency risks rendering the landscape more confusing.[60] To ignore agency risks halting the exploration on the surface.

Since the study of agency is often undertaken amid situations where choices appear curtailed, agency is most often linked to the impetus for change. As Butler asserts, agency most vividly presents itself as unauthorized uses of our bodies. Transgressing the cultural and theological messages of their day, some female preachers choose to place their bodies in prohibited spaced and to speak publicly when they had been ordered to remain silent. But agency's hidden work often lies in behaviors that conform. In accordance with the cultural and theological messages of their day, some female preachers choose to adopt socially acceptable styles of dress and to exhort from their living rooms rather than to preach from the pulpit. Through her study of Muslim women within the contemporary Egyptian mosque movement, Saba Mahmood asserts that agency should not serve as a trope for resistance but as a complex marker for the multiple ways persons determine and enact their potentiality.[61] Mahmood names agency as "a capacity for action that historically specific relations of subordination enable and create," suggesting that "agentive capacity is entailed not only in those acts that resist norms, but also in the multiple ways in which one inhabits norms."[62]

Female preachers inhabit a historically subordinate space and they continue to work amid a vast network of norms concerning the female body, the expectations placed upon preachers, a society's images of the single woman, wife, mother, or grandmother, and the specific tenets of a particular theological tradition. On one hand, female preachers have exercised tremendous structure-altering agency through preaching across history and in ways that transformed expectations about female preachers.

59. Butler, *Psychic Life of Power*, 13.

60. Ibid., 13–15. Butler articulates how structures of power bring the subject into being, continue to exert constraining influence on the subject, and are changed by the subject into different forms of power. She names this the ambivalence at the heart of agency.

61. Mahmood, "Agency," 180.

62. Ibid., 180, 186.

But alongside such dramatic actions, female preachers also have enacted their agency through conforming to social standards or theological norms about what it means to be female. Contemporary female preachers can experience both welcome and inhospitality in the pulpit, can feel at times empowered in their embodiments and at others times uneasy in their embodied presence, and often bring to the pulpit their roles as daughters, wives, partners, sisters, and/or mothers to effective and less than effective results. As one studies these preachers, conceiving of agency as the multiple ways in which one inhabits norms stays closer to female, fleshly life. It also provides a richer analysis of the meanings contained within a female preacher's decisions and behaviors.[63]

The Body on Preaching Day: Choices and the Meanings Beneath

When Rev. Rebecca Harris stood up to preach, she inhabited a body of medium height and weight, with curly black hair, and a voice strengthened by theater class to be comfortable in its range and variations. She chose to preach from the sanctuary floor, both in reaction to the authority symbolized by an evaluated pulpit and her desire to shift the church's formal culture to a slightly more informal atmosphere. Within a sanctuary she called "cavernous," she used a body that has played college soccer and given birth to children to preach without notes and often with props in a style she hoped was artful and engaging to her congregation. By Sunday morning, she had already made some choices about her body: minimum adornment, fashionable shoes, layered clothes, white alb, and stole. But the flow of worship, the messages from her body's movements, and her interactions with listeners will impact the final form of her preaching that day.

Mahmood argues, "The meaning and sense of agency cannot be fixed in advance but must emerge through an analysis of the particular concepts that enable specific modes of being, responsibility, and effectivity."[64] Within every preaching moment, particular conceptions of the preacher, what it means to preach, what kind of authority a preacher has, and the expectations around a preaching body all are at work. When women preach, other concepts join the existing ones, including prevailing notions about femininity, fashion, the expected shape of female bodies, and the social positions of race, ethnicity, age, marital status, sexual orientation, and parenthood.

63. Ibid.
64. Ibid.

Any exploration of the ways female preachers acquire a set of habitations, exercise their agency, and understand the meaning behind their choices includes such an analysis of all these modes.

How does one distinguish between being fashionable and being fashion-forward? What types of bodily presentations create what types of perceptions about a preacher? If a preacher combines the androgyny of a white alb with a distinctly feminine set of shoes, how does she experience her body while preaching, and what does the congregation perceive? How is our bodily life altered by physical factors and events beyond our control? Every female preacher encounters, as Young aptly states, a complex set of facticity and freedom. Each preacher takes up those chosen and unchosen facts in her own way. While there may be an almost infinite range of choices and meanings behind those choices, the process by which female preachers arrive at decisions concerning their bodies provides access into the modes of being, responsibility, and effectiveness at work in preaching.

In the pages that follow, the choices made by contemporary female preachers, and meanings embedded in those choices, will be explored in greater detail. These explorations will continually inquire about the habitations of the flesh demonstrated by a particular preacher, as well as how the preacher exercised her own particular mode of agency. One end goal lies in illuminating in more detail the multiple modes of being at work for all preachers. Another, more ultimate goal lies in connecting our bodily life to the Word made flesh. If preaching ushers in the transforming Word of God, then our habitations and agency can also be signs of God's Word. If preaching is about bodies, then it matters when a female body preaches. But exactly how it matters, why it matters, and to what affect is still to be fully understood.

The place to begin, though, is with Mahmood's insight that agency is enacted in both the ways women resist norms and the ways they inhabit them. For centuries, female preachers were either barred from or discouraged from preaching. Yet history bears witness to a remarkable line of female preachers. Their bodily choices in preaching demonstrate both resistance to and working within social norms. Grasping in greater detail their actions concerning their bodies and roles becomes the first step into an exploration of the female preaching body. The habitations and decisions accompanying today's preachers, while diverse and multilayered, have a history. Any understanding of preachers' current practices and decisions entails grasping the long line in which they stand. It is to this history we now turn.

CHAPTER 2

A Bodily History of Female Preaching

The Reverend Deborah Lewis worked as a lawyer and hospital administrator throughout her professional life. She litigated cases in front
of skeptical juries, walked with families facing unbearable situations, and
started her own company. Robes had fascinated her when she was a child;
choir robes, academic robes, and the solemnity of a judge's robe. Then a
series of life transitions propelled her return to church after decades of
absence, where she gradually became immersed in the community's life.
Eventually, she discerned a call to ministry. Now the pastor of a thriving
congregation, the Reverend Lewis tells people, "Clearly God had a particular robe in mind for me."

The choices Rev. Lewis made about her robed, preaching body reflected a host of habitations accompanying her gender, her African American
community, and her former professions. Within Merleau-Ponty's framework, habitations are those patterns of behavior that, through countless
repetitions, become integrated into the body's structure and serve as the
means by which the embodied self creates a coherent world.[1] Arising from
our social situatedness, habitations possess rich, multifaceted layers, which
in work in tandem to create and transmit meaning. Rev. Lewis's embodied
life drew from several distinct contexts, each providing a template through
which she organized and interpreted her behaviors. The decisions she made
about her preaching body—from clothing and vocal patterns to posture

1. Merleau-Ponty, *Phenomenology of Perception*, 104.

35

and gestures—can be understood as habitations, actions that illumine the "nexus of living meanings" associated with the female preacher.[2]

Initially trained in the law, Rev. Lewis's role as an attorney clearly influenced her physical presentation. The best sermon, from her perspective, is akin to well-honed closing remarks in which the lawyer's appearance aids the argument by lending a subtle credibility. Naming her style as conservative, she described her standard attire as a black or navy pantsuit, low-heeled shoes, subdued makeup, and a simple ensemble of earrings, wedding band, and watch. Most lawyers dress in an understated way, she elaborated, because "you want the jury to focus on your personality and not on what you are wearing." She continued, "People have to buy you in order to buy your case." Pared-down attire also minimized her femaleness. When working as an African American woman in a male-dominated field, Rev. Lewis avoided an overtly feminine appearance. Her suits were dark, her shoes flat, and her shirts devoid of frills. The approach continued in her ministry. She wore a white robe over the same pantsuits, shoes, and jewelry. Explaining her choices, she named them part of her uniform and a means by which she bolstered her authority.

Shifting to her mode of proclamation, Rev. Lewis recounted her lived experiences within the Black Church. Raised in a Baptist congregation, she was well versed in the expectations for movement and vocal rhythm within her context. "The African American tradition is more embodied," she said. "It is head movements. It is snapping my fingers." She once watched a mentor jump off the top pulpit step while preaching about soaring on eagle's wings. Knowing congregations responded to such demonstrativeness, she was pleased the Sunday she overheard a parishioner comment after her sermon, "The preacher can dance." She aims "for at least some level of verbal rhythmic responsiveness" in her sermons, often organizing the message through repetitive phrases. The practices of the African American Christian community, in a manner similar to her past legal environment, help form her embodiments. Her "stylizations of the flesh" mirror the stylization of other preachers' flesh, as she makes such preaching patterns her own.

At the same time, Rev. Lewis did far more than simply mimic the stock expectations of either the legal profession or the African American congregation. She learned the lawyer's rule of credible dress but she doesn't always adhere to its muted manifestations. While she affirmed the physical movements intertwined with African American preaching, she nuanced

2. Ibid., 175.

such activity with the assertion that "you can be deeply embodied and not move." And she remained critical of the unreflective use of certain stylistic devices. "I grew up in an old Baptist church," she reflected. "A guy could get up there and say, 'Mary had a little lamb' and the congregation would say 'yes, Lord.' There would be no content." True preaching, she insisted, required greater substance. While Rev. Lewis's bodily habitations emerged out of social contexts that helped shape her choices, she adapted communal habitations to create more individualized stylizations. Sometimes she conformed to the inherited habits. Sometimes she resisted them. Most often, she personalized the habitations over time to more fully match the needs of her body or her understanding of the task at hand. This diversity of her decisions—and the freedom to make a choice—was central to her identity. When asked to explain the reasoning behind any particular choice, Rev. Lewis consistently replied, "I'm very comfortable in my own skin. I am just me." How she arrived at "being me," though, involves a complex historical legacy of habitations.

A History of Habits

However Rev. Lewis articulated her choices about attire or movement, her decisions are not made outside of her lived experience. They are born within her context, emerging from the cultures in which she was situated. Her chosen professions shape her sense of possible dress choices. Her racial group forms her understanding of her body's potential for expression. Her gender makes her mindful of the messages she wants—and does not want—to convey about her embodied self. None of these social categories exists independently. Each is a product of a vast multitude of individual choices across time, as persons interact within several different social spheres simultaneously. Every social category's set of habitations develops out of those choices, providing the multilayered conditioning of the body integral to a functioning self.

Habitations have a history. They evolve within a community's embodied existence, as the individuals' actions to link thought and behavior become so deeply ingrained in the social web of operations that the actions appear almost magical.[3] Attempts to explain any one particular habitation illuminates how an individual's meaning-making schema flows from larger,

3. Merleau-Ponty writes, "The relationships between my decisions and my body are, in movement, magical ones" (ibid., 108).

older systems of meaning. The preacher needs to be a credible dancer, asserts Rev. Lewis, because the congregation listens to a preacher able to move. These broad systems of meaning further interact with other systems. Rev. Lewis's dual explanations about her clothing decisions represent multiple meaning-making systems at work. "You want people to forget about your clothes and concentrate on your arguments," she first asserted. But the very same attire works to increase one's credibility before a jury. She holds contradictory expectations of her embodiments, as a clothed body that both reinforces her words and fades from attention. It is a mighty task to unravel the intricate web of a long-standing, generative system at work.

Female preaching habitations have formed over time. Every female preacher has faced questions about how to clothe her body, how to speak in ways that garnished acceptance by her listeners, and how to move in ways that were authorized for a preacher. Knowing that audiences had to "buy them" in order to "buy" their preaching, female preachers in all eras of Christian history have calculated what types of embodied presentations might strengthen their legitimization. In surveying a diverse group of preachers across different eras of preaching, histories of habitations emerge. These historical habitations were crafted over time and through experimentation to enhance the authority of the female preacher, who experienced her body as an integral to her task and also a hurdle to be overcome in order to preach.

Merleau-Ponty defines a habitation as those repetitive tasks necessary to any individual's embodied involvement in her environment. Performed countless times, habitations become ingrained practices that leave "traces" upon the body, eventually enabling an individual's living mastery within her world.[4] Through her habits, the embodied person acts in certain ways in certain situations. Her behaviors are continuously refined through evolving attempts to integrate her environment in relationally meaningful ways. Analyzing the habits of the body offers a glimpse into that "core of meanings" Merleau-Ponty asserts is present in every person.[5] For the preacher, the embodied habitations attached to preaching are acquired through repeated practices of preaching. These habitations always happen amid larger, cultural conversations about the nature and definition of preaching as well as the meanings associated with male and female bodies. The

4. Grimshaw, "Working Out with Merleau-Ponty," 112.
5. Merleau-Ponty, *Phenomenology of Perception*, 173.

fleshly proficiencies female preachers gained across time proclaim something about the significance and the setbacks associated with the female preaching body.

This chapter will narrate a bodily history of female preaching by analyzing four bundles of habitations used by women to heal the gap between a contentious female body and an acceptable preacher. These four types are chosen for their representative power, as umbrella categories representing either a similar approach adopted by multiple women in one historical era or as a common approach utilized by numerous women across several historical eras. Each bundle of habitations can also be linked to at least one well-known female preacher, whose preaching expanded the forms of preaching and whose practices other preachers subsequently adopted. Since habitations are meaning-making movements, their histories are worth understanding in their own right. Because the history of our habits extends into the present, these habitational histories reveal something of the habitations still shaping the context for female preachers today.

Discovering the Historical Female Body

In recent decades, scholars have uncovered a rich but not continuous tradition of female preaching. We now know of Mary Magdalene's title as "the apostle to the apostles" and her evangelical ministry in the early church.[6] Our understanding of preaching has been widened to include the religious writings of medieval women mystics like Julian of Norwich and Hildegard of Bingen. We have accounts of the preaching ministries of eighteenth- and nineteenth-century women, especially from the Holiness and Pentecostal movements. These stories illuminate several surges of female preaching despite suppressive efforts by church leaders. Even more information exists about the twentieth-century struggles toward women's ordination, including collections of women's sermons. Taken all together these records demonstrate that women preached in almost every era of Christian history. From the traces of these manuscripts we glean something of their sermons. From the entries of their journals and other historical records we learn of the challenges to preach in eras that barred female preaching. We know that the trajectories of female preaching are long, deep, and wide, even as our

6. Jansen, "Maria Magdalena," 57–96.

reconstructions of these histories struggle against the gaps between preachers, the silencing of women, and the outright erasure of their stories.[7]

Yet we have only begun to build a physical history of the female preacher.[8] One hurdle lies in the process of historical retrieval. Certain things—like sermon manuscripts and journal entries—can be discovered and analyzed. Other information—like a preacher's experience of her body or a congregation's impression about a preacher's gestures, postures, and voice—are more difficult to recover. It is hard to gain insight into the embodied decisions of female preachers from historical documents beyond the occasional reference to her body and the still-life picture of the preacher. It is almost impossible to know with certainty how a female preacher conceived of or sought to utilize her own body. For all that scholars have unearthed about the tremendous legacy of female preaching, we are still exploring the choices women made about their bodies and the implications of those choices for themselves, their congregations, and their preaching.

A second hurdle in exploring the physicality of the female preacher comes from the theological concepts attached to women's bodies. From the beginning of Christianity, the female body has been a site of intense scrutiny and ongoing suspicion. Biblical admonishments required women to be silent in church.[9] Women were formally excluded from preaching at an early juncture in the church's development. Through the centuries, religious authorities sought close control over female bodies, often tagging them with tropes associated with archetypal saint, best represented in Mary the mother of Jesus, or with an archetypal sinner, often symbolized by Mary Magdalene, who, on the basis of little evidence, was given a promiscuous past.[10] The female who sought to preach was named out of place, inferior, unclean, or beautifully but dangerously alluring.[11] More than one bishop in the Middle Ages argued that a woman should not preach because "her appearance would provoke lascivious thoughts."[12] John Cotton, the seventeenth-century New England Puritan, suggested, "a woman who was

7. See Brekus, *Strangers and Pilgrims*, 4–10, 15–16.

8. Two notable exceptions to this claim arise in the rich descriptive and analytical windows to the female preaching body found in Brekus, *Strangers and Pilgrims*, 88–113, and Best, *Passionately Human*.

9. Two often-quoted biblical passages are 1 Cor 14:34 and 1 Tim 2:11–12.

10. Brekus, *Strangers and Pilgrims*, 41.

11. Lawless, *Holy Women*, 226.

12. Muessig, "Prophecy and Song," 154; Kim, *Women Preaching*, 53.

allowed to speak or testify in the church might soon prove a seducer."[13]
These seductive suspicions existed alongside paradoxical suggestions that
women who preached were somehow less female. President-to-be James
Garfield confessed that there was "something about a woman speaking in
public that unsexes her" in his mind.[14] The women who did preach, therefore, risked the skeptical gazes of observers searching for her alluring powers and listeners who questioned her femininity or her representation of
the gospel. Bearing a host of semiotic and symbolic meanings, the female
preaching body was a controversial body, over-studied amid anxiety about
its potential danger and under-studied for its powerful agency. The task of
overcoming the female body's contention has proven difficult, rendering it
arduous to explore female preaching embodiment in more neutral or nuanced ways.

A History Narrated through Habitations

The female preacher of centuries past recognized the dissension accompanying her embodiment. Occasionally, she attempted to diffuse suspicion by
offering alternate interpretations of her body, so glaringly different than a
male preaching body. In these instances, preachers portrayed bodily barriers as bodily assets. A woman riddled with physical ailments, possibly
triggered by the societal distress surrounding her public performance,
could respond to the preaching manual's mandate to look "healthy with
radiant color" with claims that it was precisely through physical "weakness
and fatigue [that] God grabbed their attention."[15] Aware that her shorter
height necessitated a step stool at the pulpit, another preacher proclaimed,
"I'm a little but powerful handmaiden of the Lord."[16] But words alone could
not heal the discomfort generated by female preachers. Verbal messages
only went so far. Instead female preachers developed habitations aimed at
crafting new spaces for their speech. Recognizing the resistance to their
preaching, female preachers, through trial and error, experimented with
their physicality in efforts to gain access to the pulpit.

13. Brekus, *Strangers and Pilgrims*, 30.

14. Muir, *Petticoats in the Pulpit*, 98.

15. The advice for robust preaching performances comes from Walters, "Body in
the Pulpit," 447. The woman's response is found in Lawless, *Handmaidens of the Lord*,
xviii–xix.

16. Lawless, *Handmaidens of the Lord*, xviii–xix.

Looking across the history of female preaching, four broad sets of habitations coalesce as avenues through which women sought legitimacy as preachers. These habitations vary within different historical, cultural, and theological settings, as well as by the nuances of particular situations and personalities. But they all formed from a common recognition that the female preacher was not wholly welcomed. The first bundle of habitations depicts women who responded to the messages of being unfit for the pulpit by attempting to rise above their bodies while they preached. Distinguishing spiritual authority from fleshly life, *transcending women* emphasized the gift of the Holy Spirit and minimized the body's role in preaching. A second bundle of habitations describes the female preacher who answered the barriers placed upon her preaching by adopting signs of maleness into her embodiment. These *women who act like men* chose to emulate the attributes ascribed to their male colleagues in their dress, voice, or movements. A third set of habitations clusters around women who closely linked dress, voice, and movements to cultural images of the impeccably moral woman. These *virtuous women* typically exemplified sacrificial, loving wives and mothers but included any females who projected irreproachable femininity. A final habitational group represents women who relied upon behaviors that violated socially accepted boundaries surrounding femininity, often in ways their listeners found sexually provocative. These *transgressing women* broke the rules about how women might look or act while they preach and created a new habitation in the process. Taken as a whole group, the women who transcend, the women who act like men, the virtuous women, and the women who transgress depict some distinctive habits accompanying female preaching, the diverse stylizations of the flesh possible within their proclamation.

Each bundle of habitations represents an approach to embodied life. With only four broad sets, they cannot encapsulate all the bodily possibilities available to female preachers. Instead they serve as tools constructed specifically for the purpose of analyzing how women use their bodies, with full knowledge that many other sets of habitations are possible. No one actual performance will fit any one theoretical approach. Nor will any one woman be a precise combination of characteristics from multiple models. Instead every woman will exceed the habitations, even while conforming to certain aspects of them. Hence, the habitations serve as vehicles to illumine the complex social performances happening within preaching bodies. The bundles further reveal the chasms existing between theoretical constructs and the always enfleshed preacher, between the established sets of habitations and the still evolving ones. It is in the space between the gaps that we learn about our shared existence as embodied preachers.

At the same time, these bundles of habits are not crafted arbitrarily. They grow out of a close historical analysis of actual preaching women across time and place. They are rooted in social situations, cultural messages, and particular lives. Each set provides greater insight into a time period, community of women, or theological perspective. Telling their history can illumine the combination of habitations at work within contemporary preachers, who are still being formed by social and historical realities and are still retooling their embodied practices for new configurations of preaching.

Not the Body but the Spirit: Habits of Transcendence

When reading a wide selection of call narratives by female preachers, a common threefold pattern surfaces among the variety of individual experiences. The women's stories start with an inward inclination to preach.[17] Women resist this nascent call, emphatically suppressing the urge or emphasizing the prohibitions preventing them from preaching. During this second phase, women could suffer physical distress as the resistance takes root bodily. Finally, often after years of self-doubt, women experience the Holy Spirit entering their struggle, overwhelming their objections and propelling them to preach. As they described this third phase, women speak of the Spirit invading their embodied existence or superseding their bodily life. The Spirit becomes the source of their authority to preach and provides a rationale for minimizing their female bodies. Filled with the Spirit, these transcending preachers stress that their flesh faded away as the Spirit took root.

Two historical streams of thought supported the habits of transcendence: theological tenets promoting the separation of flesh and spirit and cultural messages denigrating the female body. Early Christian tradition distinguished the spirit from the flesh, associating the flesh with bound, earthly existence and the spirit with the realms of heaven and holiness. Empowering the spirit and not the flesh, the Holy Spirit authorized an individual to preach. Theologians who supported the Spirit's capacity to

17. See Brekus, *Strangers and Pilgrims*; Kienzle and Walker, *Women Preachers*; Humez, *Gifts of Power*.

transform persons into preachers often argued that gender was attached only to the flesh.[18] Such a theological position held special importance for women, who were well versed in cultural messages that linked female bodies to a brute, base body unfit for the pulpit.[19] By emphasizing the Spirit's authorizing power given to them through ecstatic or mystical experiences, women circumvented the bodily-based objections to their preaching. They neutralized the fear of female sexuality by stressing the Spirit's purifying capacity, which emptied the body of its desires. Thus, transcending women viewed themselves as containers for God, in which their physical form was immaterial to proclamation.

Flesh-denying, spirit-emphasizing practices were evident in the medieval church, as female mystics engaged in physical disciplines such as fasting, sexual abstinence, and cutting off their hair.[20] In this era, the church lifted up religious leaders like Rose Viterbo, whose public preaching during the thirteenth century was credited to a "purity of mind and body" born of the chastening presence of the Spirit.[21] Similar practices were evidenced in post-Reformation movements that contained female preachers. An early supporter of female preachers, the Quaker tradition affirmed the notion that the Spirit granted women gender-transcending capacities. Female Quaker preachers dressed in simple, unadorned gowns, typically either dark colored or white. Their dress communicated plainness, moderation, or "the stripping away of . . . carnal indulgence."[22] The same attire would go on to assume different meaning in later eras, but it originated as a method by which to present a gender-less presence. By decreasing the body's noticeability, especially its distinctive female features, these women signaled that the Spirit served as the authority of their preaching.

One example of the transcending habitations emerged in the figure of Jemima Wilkinson. An itinerant preacher during the Revolutionary War period, Wilkinson's preaching ministry in the New England and mid-Atlantic areas began with her miraculous experience of the Spirit choosing to dwell in her body. Following a weeklong, severe illness, she awoke to claim her female self had died and been resurrected as the Public Universal

18. King, "Prophetic Power," 25.

19. Brekus, *Strangers and Pilgrims*, 52–53.

20. Several historians note this trend. See Flinders, *Enduring Grace*; Brenon, "Voice of the Good Woman," 114–33.

21. Muessig, "Prophecy and Song," 148–49.

22. Larson, *Daughters of Light*, 41.

Friend.[23] Naming her resurrected body as a "tabernacle" for God, Wilkinson asserted that she was no longer a woman but a spirit divinely inspired to preach. She referred to herself as Public Universal Friend, or simply Friend, for the rest of her life and insisted her followers not use any pronouns, male or female, in writings about her. She advocated celibacy, claiming the desires of the flesh were absent from her reborn spirit. She kept her body veiled behind flowing clerical gowns that "fastened at the neck and hid all but her hands, feet, and face."[24] Enjoying much prominence as a preacher, Jemima Wilkinson symbolized how life in the Spirit enabled the preaching of one (genderless) woman.

Wilkinson's assertion of an embodied self overwhelmed by God is replicated, in far more mild ways, by the preacher who claims divine authority behind her speech and who, intuiting her femaleness may hinder her acceptance, presents her female body as an extra in her preaching. Rev. Lewis interprets her well-covering, plain, dark attire as choices designed to deflect attention away from her physicality. Rev. Erin Robinson seeks to dress in a manner that "allows everyone to forget that I am a female." Rev. Laura Martin characterizes her preaching as times of "God using me," and asserts, "My body is the last thing I'm thinking about." In these moments, the preacher encourages congregations and herself to forget her embodiment.

The habitations of transcendence may appear, even temporarily, successful. It is hard to dispute claims of divine authority. But habitations that dismiss a person's inescapable body will prove more difficult to sustain and more costly to a preacher's embodied life. Divorced from the "body that is me," preachers may lose the network of meanings arising from a lived body. Wilkinson's efforts to focus upon the Spirit rendered her body devoid of its particularity and publicly discredited from any preaching involvement. Furthermore, female preachers who attempt transcendence inadvertently affirm the body's ever-involvement in preaching. They enact transcendence, paradoxically, through careful attention to the body's dress, posture, and adornments. Jemima Wilkinson's long gown demonstrates how women who present a Spirit-infused body, in effect, employ the body in the service of its own disappearance.

The body is always with the preacher; the preacher's body is always preaching. The female preachers across history who stressed the transcending power of the Spirit also contended with the solid reality of their flesh.

23. Brekus, *Strangers and Pilgrims*, 80–97.
24. Ibid., 87.

It is worth noticing how many eighteenth- and nineteenth-century female preachers who claimed the Spirit compelled them to preach also reported prolonged periods of bodily distress including nightmares, tremors, paralysis, and debilitating illnesses.[25] Similar accounts of physical suffering can be found in the narratives of medieval women mystics. These material manifestations survive to the present day. In her studies of contemporary Pentecostal female preachers, Elaine Lawless notes multiple instances of backaches, headaches, unexplained pain, and chronic weariness.[26] Whatever habits of transcendence endure, the body remains present during preaching.

Although Jemima Wilkinson never wavered from her assertion that a genderless spirit had replaced her female self, most historical descriptions remarked upon the maleness of her appearance. Her long, loose cloaks mimicked the clothes of male clergy. She strengthened this connection by knotting a man's handkerchief at her neck and styling her hair in the looser, more flowing fashions associated with the masculine style.[27] In this way, Jemima Wilkinson relied upon more than one set of habitations to craft her space to preach. Insisting she preached as a spirit, she also drew heavily from a second bundle of habits, molding her body to look like a man.

The Male-Like Woman: Female Bodies in Masculine Forms

In the middle to late Middle Ages, iconography appeared in Western European churches naming Mary Magdalene as the apostle to the apostles, illustrating her proclamation to the disciples of Christ's resurrection and her subsequent missionary activity to preach the gospel.[28] Although every picture was unique, all of the icons granted this first apostle a new level of authority. Her body appeared comparable to male preachers. In some, she stood adorned in preaching robes rather than traditional female attire. In many, she bore the golden aureola, reserved for early church preachers. In another, she spoke from the pulpit.[29] But like icons of Catherine of Alexandria and Rose of Viterbo from roughly the same time period, it was

25. Muir, *Petticoats in the Pulpit*, 58; Brekus, *Strangers and Pilgrims*, 87, 165, 184; Lawless, *Holy Women*, xvii, 29, 93.

26. Lawless, *Handmaidens of the Lord*, xvii, 29.

27. Brekus, *Strangers and Pilgrims*, 87.

28. Jansen, "Maria Magdalena," 67.

29. Ibid., 72–73.

the depiction of her gestures that most identified her as a preacher of the church. All three female figures were drawn employing the standard hand gestures of preachers; right hand raised and index finger pointed upward while the left hand, palm open, extended outward at waist level.[30] While her authority as a preacher drew strength from multiple sources, including sermons and historical writings, these devotional pictures conferred male-like attributes on Mary. She entered the preaching space reserved for men with the symbols associated with male preachers.

Given a history of exclusion, it seems natural that female preachers would garner recognition by emulating male counterparts. Stepping into a male-dominated arena, women had virtually no other preaching forms to observe and broad encouragement to revere masculine traits.[31] Masculine traits would strengthen their visibility, acceptance, and authority. Furthermore, the theological tradition of distinguishing between spirit and flesh, with gender understood to be inscribed on the flesh, prompted assertions that Spirit-inspired preachers have entered a sexless realm.[32] One medieval sect even went so far as to claim that holy women become males in the afterlife.[33] Although used in support of transcending habitations, the idea that women could abandon their femininity extended into an operative plasticity of gender for anyone called by the Spirit to preach. Rather than transcending her body, a woman could choose to distance herself from her femininity in order to re-represent herself as male.

The most easily accessible avenue for male-like habitations came through a preacher's choice of clothing. History witnesses to the host of women who copied male dress in order to gain access to professions previously barred to them.[34] Early female preachers utilized the long, flowing gowns standard for preaching. Such male-mimicking tactics carry into modern times, as female preachers continue wearing clothing associated with men, including preaching albs, academic robes, and even their own versions of the 1980s power suit.

30. Rusconi, "Women's Sermons," 173, 191.

31. Brekus, *Strangers and Pilgrims*, 52-53.

32. King, "Prophetic Power," 25.

33. Brenon, "Voice of the Good Woman," 119-20.

34. Brekus writes, "Clothing has functioned as one of the primary means of representing sexual difference and perpetuating sexual inequality. It is not surprising then, that women who have wanted to increase their status have appropriated the most visible signs of men's power: their pants, vests, shirts and even clerical robes" (*Strangers and Pilgrims*, 87-88).

Another avenue available for female preachers involves male-like mannerisms or relational styles. As previously noted, Jemima Wilkinson combined her conceptual arguments about becoming Public Universal Friend with a decidedly male demeanor. Her strong authoritarian leadership prompted critics to accuse her of acting like a man.[35] Similar charges were directed toward Jarena Lee, a nineteenth-century evangelist who had to address accusations that she was "a man dressed in female clothes."[36] These historical female preachers played with their physical presentations and personas in a way that troubled their gender identity. Like transcending women, they minimized overtly feminine traits but toward a different end. Rather than arguing their bodies were absent or irrelevant to their preaching, they sought preaching embodiments that fulfilled what Wallace Best calls the template of "manliness" often used to judge both male and female preachers.[37]

One prominent female who played with the masculinity of her preaching role was Elder Lucy Smith, a popular preacher in Chicago during the first half of the twentieth century. Smith established All Nations Pentecostal Church and subsequent multi-church conference. Her "down-home" speech and emotionally exuberant worship resonated among the multitude of southern African Americans who flooded the city during the Great Migration.[38] Ministering during an era in which women preachers were gaining prominence, Smith encountered the common charge that female preachers "were usurping positions that rightfully belonged to men."[39] One element of such "masculinist conception[s] of ministry and the discourse of 'masculine' and 'feminine' so intrinsic to it," asserts Best, was the attention placed upon "black women preachers' bodies [that] invited speculation about their sexuality."[40] Smith's embodied response to her new urban environment came in portraying a "complicated" sexuality and actions that "consciously perform[ed] 'mannishness.'"[41]

Elder Smith displayed "mannishness" through a paradoxical blending of male and female roles. Smith was often seen "embracing motherliness

35. Ibid.
36. Ibid., 179.
37. Best, *Passionately Human*, 155.
38. Ibid., 151, 171, 181.
39. Ibid., 154.
40. Ibid., 155.
41. Ibid., 156.

while rejecting conventional domesticity."[42] She was called "Mother" in multiple contexts, with observers naming her "mother-image to the drifting black masses."[43] Her official title, though, was "Overseer" of the church, a term with masculine implications. She repeatedly insisted God had called her out of the kitchen and into the pulpit.[44] Descriptions of Smith given in publications of her time included words like plain and homely, as well as "somewhat mannish, overweight, and hoarse."[45]

Knowing that public attention honed in on their physical appearance, African American female preachers in the early twentieth century, Best argues, typically worked to deflect away such attention. Elder Smith's imposing physical presence made such deflection difficult, but not impossible.[46] Dark skinned and quite tall, Smith weighed, before an illness, over three hundred pounds.[47] Surviving photographs show her standing behind a pulpit dressed in a long, white dress with wide collar. Her only jewelry was a gold pocket watch hanging around her neck from a simple black cord. Her hair was kept short, straight, and close to her head. Through both appearance and actions, Elder Smith kept her femaleness offstage. She eliminated allusions to an active sexuality by leaving her husband at home. She dressed without adornments. She answered critics who asserted preaching is a man's calling by functioning as a compelling worship leader and church administrator in a well-known and well-attended church. Although never renouncing her femaleness, Smith led with the efficiency, confidence, and competency previously associated with male pastor-preachers.[48]

The habitations around preaching like a man might more accurately be phrased as the preacher who is neither fully male nor fully female. When analyzing Smith's appearance, Best notes, "Christian, black women preachers aimed to detract attention from their bodies, sex, and sexuality not by denying their gender but by rendering themselves ambiguous."[49] Living in contexts in which gender, race, and culture all intersected, African

42. Ibid.
43. Ibid., 160.
44. Ibid., 161.
45. Ibid., 155.
46. Ibid., 159.
47. Ibid., 150–51.
48. Ibid., 150.
49. Ibid., 156.

American female preachers "complicated the notion of femaleness."[50] Elder Smith drew from her physical robustness, vocal strength, and commanding presence to utilize forms of authority traditionally linked to male preachers. She also wore the white dresses adopted by many female preachers and nurtured a motherly persona within her congregation. Appearing neither entirely male nor entirely female, she performed "mannishness" in a selective way, picking and choosing from a variety of masculine and feminine traits as they best served her purposes. We cannot know how Elder Smith experienced this duality of performed personas. It may be that her use of male-like traits fit well with her self-understanding. It could also be that her success as one who "preached like a man" encouraged her instrumental uses of her body in that direction, even as the uses grated against her own sensibility. Mixing female and male forms, receiving both praise and denigration, Smith lived amid contradictory habitations.

The habitations surrounding women who utilize male attributes weave a steady trail through the history of female preaching. Such practices remain a viable resource for contemporary women. Rev. Lewis chose to wear a pantsuit—and not a skirt—each Sunday morning. She kept her hair short. Possessing a vocal range in the lower octaves, Rev. Lewis's speech was called a deep melody by a former congregant, a characterization that implied a strength typically found in male voices. Like Elder Smith, Rev. Lewis is an African American preacher serving an African American congregation. While the habitations of maleness may be more readily available to certain African American women, they also may be thrust upon them, especially in a racist culture that links many manifestations of femininity to white women.

Although adopting a more masculine persona can serve an individual preacher or work well within a particular situation, these habitations possess real limitations. Elder Lucy Smith never escaped questions about her gender or the true basis of her pastoral authority. Looking like a man left the problem of preaching as a female unsolved. While contemporary preachers have greater freedom in adopting male and female characteristics, and wider options in how to express the complexity inherent in gendered life, habitations that require a person to relinquish one aspect of her identity truncate the fullest exploration of embodied existence. An aspect of Elder Smith's paradoxical presentations surely rested in her efforts to navigate the "cultural and social inscriptions" placed upon her body, reminding us that

50. Ibid.

the truncating of embodiment can come from cultural rather than personal motivations.[51] Yet even the women who adopted more masculine associated behaviors or appearances were recognized as female. For all the claims of being a male dressed in female clothes, Jarena Lee is counted among the mighty witnesses of female preachers. So are Jemima Wilkinson and Elder Lucy Smith.

The Virtuous Women: The Body Beyond Reproach

In the first two sets of habitations, female preachers sought avenues by which to deflect the attention directed toward their bodies. In contrast, the next two bundles of habitations, although vastly different in scope, shifted toward affirming the preacher's enfleshment. Rather than emulating male characteristics or transcending the body, women who employed these final habitations found ways to preach within their femaleness. The third set of habitations relied upon cultural notions of the virtuous woman. In the fourth habitation female preachers experimented with practices that violated culturally acceptable female forms and behaviors.

The conceptual basis for a woman's authority to preach underwent dramatic shifts during the nineteenth century. Until this point, female preachers had justified their public ministries through authorities outside themselves, authorities such as the Holy Spirit or the borrowed legitimacy of male preachers. But nineteenth-century female preachers faced a changing notion of womanhood. Rather than being cast as the more base or immoral gender, women increasingly were viewed as the more praiseworthy sex, whose moral superiority granted them the authority to preach.[52] Purity, once attained only through habits of transcendence, now became closely associated with the female's embodied life. Linking outward behavior to one's inner character, the properly presented and impeccably behaved woman served as a cultural model.[53] Once preaching despite their femininity, women now began to preach because of it.[54]

---

51. Ibid., 150.

52. Brekus, *Strangers and Pilgrims*, 119–20. See also Edwards, *History of Preaching*, 567–71. Edwards offers an account of female preaching during the Holiness Movement.

53. For analysis of women's embodiment of this particular cultural model, see Halttunen, *Confidence Men and Painted Women*.

54. Brekus, *Strangers and Pilgrims*, 160.

The virtuous woman habitations presented a *female* preacher, who exhibited the new social conceptions of womanhood through her attire, mannerisms, and demeanor. These embodiments were reserved almost exclusively for upper- and middle-class white women. They were modestly dressed, possessed voices described as "pure, unstudied eloquence," and employed the refined movements linked with women of high social standing.[55] The Quaker style of simple, unadorned gowns had evolved into the standard clothes for female evangelical preachers. Some women added small adornments such as a piece of lace or a ruffle on the collar, which introduced a more feminine look. The cultural conventions governing clothing and behavior explicitly connected the virtuous woman to her familial roles as a wife and mother. Female preachers utilized titles like "Mother" or "Sister" even as they extended their preaching scope from the insular family into more public contexts.[56] Often they preached—whether or not they termed it preaching—from their homes, symbolizing the domestic origins of their spiritual leadership. These shifts can be documented not only in female preachers, but also in women involved in a variety of nineteenth-century reform movements, including abolition, temperance, and suffrage. Through attire, mannerisms, and adherence to proper boundaries, the virtuous woman embodied a certain goodness that symbolized spiritual authority. And thereby she gained acceptance as a preacher.

One illustration of the virtuous habitations came in the preaching ministry of Catherine Booth. Spanning thirty years, from 1860 to 1890, Booth preached throughout the world as part of the husband-wife team that founded the Salvation Army. Born into a British Methodist household and married to a Methodist preacher, Booth matured amid the Holiness movement of the late nineteenth century. With deep inclinations toward social reform and spiritual sanctification, her preaching regularly touched upon the need for piety in word and deed. Booth coupled her passionate moral vision with examples of her life as a wife and mother of eight children. She wore the Evangelical preacher's typical dark, simple gown with a white ruffle at the neck and a bonnet on her head. Even when arguing her potentially controversial belief in women's natural right to preach, she delivered her words in a body described as becomingly attired, graceful in form, and pleasing in manners.[57]

55. Larson, *Daughters of Light*, 238.

56. Brekus, *Strangers and Pilgrims*, 105. Brekus focuses upon Ann Lee. Another example would come with Sister Aimee Semple McPherson.

57. Green, *Catherine Booth*, 126, 191.

Her writings have been preserved, as have outside observations of her preaching. Thus scholars know Booth experienced a divine summons to preach as an adult. While struggling to justify her call, she eventually rejected the prevailing belief that female preaching was an exceptional activity made possible only by the Holy Spirit. She argued instead for a biblical mandate of gender equality, insisting that women, like men, possess an innate ability to preach. The Galatians text she referenced, "In Christ there is neither male nor female," could support transcending habits, but Booth utilized it to argue that Christ dwells in both men and women.[58] "It is wrong," she wrote, "to thereby assume that a woman is not *by nature* fitted to preach."[59] After preaching for her ill husband one evening, Booth commented that there is nothing either "unnatural or immodest in a Christian woman, becomingly attired, appearing on a platform or in a pulpit."[60] Early in her preaching ministry, a local newspaper published an illustration of the preacher Booth dressed in her husband's clothes.[61] While Booth lamented the portrayal, her own bodily presentation responded to its underlying concerns. She dressed as the middle-class, educated, refined woman she was. She presented an irreproachable woman. The virtuousness that marked her as a woman facilitated her preaching.

Amid this impeccable performance, Booth also authorized the formation of the Hallelujah Lads and Lasses. This extension arm of the Salvation Army aimed to enlist young men and women for an evangelistic street ministry. The group practiced an enthusiastic, and at times outrageous, style of worship through hymns set to show tunes and dramatic presentations complete with costumes, instruments, and dancing.[62] One well-known Hallelujah Lass, Happy Ezra, earned a reputation for preaching in dress styles her listeners found provocative, with flowing, long hair and a fiddle in her hand.[63] While they eventually received uniforms, the Lads and Lasses consistently pushed the boundaries of acceptability. They embraced commercial entertainment, associated with prostitutes, and received accusations of uncleanliness or immorality.[64] By inverting socially unacceptable images

58. Gal 3:28 NSRV.
59. Green, *Catherine Booth*, 118, emphasis added.
60. Ibid., 126, 136.
61. Ibid., 127–28.
62. Walker, "Chaste and Fervid Eloquence," 297.
63. Ibid.
64. Ibid., 298.

into gospel messages and exemplifying anything but virtuous behaviors, they embodied all that Booth herself did not.

Notwithstanding her work to create the Hallelujah Lads and Lasses, Catherine Booth endures as a symbol of the virtuous female preacher. Demonstrating a bundle of habitations through which women preached as women, she illumines the strengths and constraints embedded in culturally sanctioned embodiments of femininity. Virtuous habitations inevitably limited other expressions of femininity. While utilizing these habitations to speak out upon controversial topics, virtuous preachers maintained the physical attributes of decorum.[65] The virtuous preacher was not the single, sexually available woman or the dancing, shouting, fiery preacher. Contemporary female preachers experience the legacy of these virtuous habitations. While they may not receive such strong admonishments about how to be female—although such admonishments do happen—women wrestle with a legacy of acceptable and unacceptable forms in the pulpit. They may worry if their dress is cut too low or their hair looks too long, flowing, and unfettered. They may field comments about not looking like a minister or being too attractive for the pulpit. Many preachers added stories to their sermons arising from their lived experiences as wives and mothers in hopes of increasing listeners' trust. Their ongoing efforts to satisfy expectations associated with being virtuous enough to preach foreshadow the continuing suspicions surrounding being a *female* preacher. In adhering to social conventions, women acknowledge an alternate path: transgressing the boundaries as they preach.

The Transgressors: Breaching the Boundaries

The fourth and final set of habitations emerged from the long-standing suspicions linked to the female preaching body. While the virtuous preacher crafted her space by adhering to conventional models of being female, transgressing preachers carved out preaching opportunities through outrageous or exaggerated behaviors. They preached in unexpected, often provocative, spaces or with wild abandon involving dramatic physical movements. Relying upon the ways female preaching has been characterized as an act beyond the acceptable, they took strength from defying rather than conforming to social norms. Their controversial behaviors could and

65. See Zink-Sawyer, *From Preachers to Suffragists.*

did invoke the fears listeners associated with a female preacher, especially the danger of her sexuality.

Drawing from both the Medieval and Reformation eras, a composite image emerged of the transgressing preacher. She spoke on the streets, shouted at her detractors, and embraced rather than feared the labels of harlot or heretic.[66] At times she preached in scanty clothing, in clothing associated with the bedroom, or even without clothes to bring attention to her message.[67] These scandalous tactics most readily appeared at the beginning of a new historical era, through the female members of emergent religious sects. Women preachers among the Waldensians reportedly hurled insults at bishops who tried to contain their preaching and boasted of their freedom within the movement's missionary activity.[68] Among eighteenth- and nineteenth-century evangelists, female preachers were known for similar contentiousness as well as for shouting, jumping, groaning, or weeping as they spoke.[69] The behaviors of the Hallelujah Lasses can be understood as transgressing habitations, as these women wore revealing attire, used boisterous music, and occupied open, public spaces at unexpected times.

Whenever a woman's public behavior was scrutinized, her sexuality became suspect. Preachers within this cluster of habitations were viewed less as wives or mothers and more as sexual beings and potential lovers. The bishops subduing the Waldensian preachers concluded the women were prostitutes.[70] Other female preachers were derided as strange women or witches.[71] The Hallelujah Lasses were denounced through a "particularly sexualized form of abuse and ridicule."[72] Even when the preacher's transgressions were distinct from alluring behaviors, the fact that she violated a boundary created the risk of being judged through the lens of her sexuality.

Over time, the habits of transgression were able to change the guiding images of a woman's proper place, voice, appearance, or behavior. Transgressing women received much attention and, in this sense, their efforts widened the space of all female preachers. As they shouted, danced, walked

66. Walker, "Chaste and Fervid Eloquence," 296–97.

67. See Kienzle, "Prostitute-Preacher"; Brenon, "Voice of the Good Woman"; Edwards, *History of Preaching*, 561–63.

68. Kienzle, "Prostitute-Preacher," 99–100.

69. Brekus, *Strangers and Pilgrims*, 55.

70. Kienzle, "Prostitute-Preacher," 101.

71. Brekus, *Strangers and Pilgrims*, 97.

72. Walker, "Chaste and Fervid Eloquence," 297.

the streets, and wore fewer clothes, they broke through cultural rules about how a woman must present herself. What was viewed as unacceptable behavior in one era—jumping, dancing, or weeping—became acceptable in subsequent eras. From this perspective, transgressing actions appear as exercises of agency, instances in which women freely chose how they presented and used their bodies. But a closer analysis reveals a more complicated scenario. As Brekus rightly points out, in previous centuries "women used their bodies to act out the emotions that could not—or would not—be put into words."[73] Modern-day Pentecostal female preachers exhibit similar movements of dancing, crying, shouting, and clapping. Yet they do so in congregations that do not allow them to preach from the pulpit's proper space.[74] The preacher that twirls, cries, shouts, and dances may be as bound by restrictive habitations as the virtuous preacher. Furthermore, habitations solidify over time. Transgressive behaviors lose their outrageous quality as the listening community grows accustomed to a preacher's repeated provocations. The woman who continuously employs the same actions risks becoming, like a virtuous preacher, restrained in her established role.

Aimee Semple McPherson offered one portrait of a transgressing preacher. Raised in a Salvation Army household, McPherson's career began as a traveling evangelist in the early twentieth century. Photographs of McPherson taken in 1918 show a stately woman, with a plain face and dark hair pulled up upon her head. She wore the traditional Pentecostal attire of a lengthy white dress with a wide collar, accompanied by a black cape draped across her shoulders. While remaining true to a conservative, evangelical tradition in the content of her sermons, she experimented with her embodiment throughout her preaching years, reaching for styles that broke boundaries and rewrote preaching rules. Undergoing a noticeable physical transformation, the preacher who first appeared akin to Catherine Booth gradually came to look more like a Hollywood star.

Having initially displayed habitations of the virtuous woman, McPherson altered her habits as she built a Los Angeles-based preaching ministry. Viewing preaching as a performance on a dramatic stage, she adopted the city's entertainment methods by adding costumes, props, and music to her sermons that formed large-scale, multisensory spectacles.[75] In such "illustrated sermons," McPherson donned costumes; appearing as a country

73. Brekus, *Strangers and Pilgrims*, 47.

74. Lawless, "Introducing the Issue of Blood," 3.

75. Sutton, *Aimee Semple McPherson*, 71–72.

milkmaid in "The Story of My Life" and a police officer in "Arrested for Speeding."[76] Breaking from widely held expectations about proper preaching, her costumes were jovial, fashionable, and rendered her body another prop in the sermon. She also possessed a magnetic personality, which led many listeners to comment on her powerful charisma.[77] Experimenting with preaching forms, she drew attention to her physical presence.

As her preaching ministry grew, her femaleness became central to her presentation. Known as "Sister Aimee," McPherson was the divorced mother of two children. She tackled sexually explicit biblical passages, cast herself as the bride of Christ, and once preached a sermon entitled "Be My Valentine."[78] Although lauded by fans, her critics labeled the preaching magnetism a hypnotic, sexually charged allure.[79] Her body changed. Once a dark-haired, plump, plain-clothed woman noted for being "physically nondescript," McPherson lost weight, lightened the color and shortened the style of her hair, and wore fashion-conscious clothes.[80] She posed for a photograph in a white evening gown. Through preaching topics and physical characteristics, McPherson presented herself as an appealing—and available—female preacher. Similar to the tactics of the virtuous woman, she relied upon her embodied persona as a preaching tool. But unlike the preacher who projected a purified version of wife and mother, McPherson placed her sexuality in plain view. Her positioning of herself as an object of sexual desire became a trademark of her preaching.

The lines between McPherson's femaleness, sexuality, body, and preaching were not necessarily clear cut. Her habitations revealed the contradictions of her various approaches to embodiment. While McPherson did break barriers in how preachers could preach, she was not the first preacher to manipulate cultural or sexual tropes for her own ends. Furthermore, her decisions about her physique, dress, and body techniques reflected a complex intertwining of herself and her culture. McPherson's radical change in appearance can be viewed as a growing comfort in expressing her sexuality or as a compulsive conforming to changing notions of female beauty or both. She pushed the boundaries of acceptability in female preaching just as she symbolized adherence to new standards of womanhood. Similar

76. Ibid., 75, 86.
77. Ibid., 55.
78. Ibid., 15, 55–58.
79. Ibid., 55.
80. Ibid., 127, 158–60.

complications existed in her choices around costumes. To don a policeman's uniform may be to mimic Hollywood, to act like a man, or to bring a wider range of her body into the pulpit. Her sense of the dramatic—and her explicit use of her body—served to both empower her preaching and confine her identity. Just as generations of preachers before her used their bodies to express what they could not speak aloud, McPherson's preaching body hinted at larger cultural, theological, and homiletical conversations. Her habitations, then, brought to the forefront the ways the embodied preacher responds to and recreates her world, in which every behavior has rich layers of agential meaning.

Today's female preacher inhabits a preaching landscape in which a variety of forms of femininity are accepted. The habits of transgressive femininity are not only less explosive but even routinized. Contemporary female preachers do put on costumes and use their bodies as props. Rev. Lewis began one sermon seated behind the church's back pew, impersonating the injured man on the road between Jerusalem and Jericho. Another preacher once wore an animation costume for the children's message. Women also encountered choices about whether or not to bring any markers of sexuality into their preaching. These discernments accompanied decisions about high-heeled shoes, dangling jewelry, and loosely flowing hair, among others. Often such efforts sprang from a pull toward a fuller embodiment of themselves. Such decisions can include some transgression—and are salutatory. With the witness of former transgressing preachers as a foundation, female preachers track their own debatable boundaries, a moving target which can encourage experimentation, teach them their limits, and enliven their preaching presence.

Historical Habitations: Cultivating Intentionality

Questions about the intersection between embodiment and empowerment lurk within all four habitations, as the transcenders, the transgressors, the women who modeled feminine virtue, and the women who acted like men strove to craft a space to preach with a female body. Each habitation represents a different approach to presenting one's female embodiment and a different mode for accessing a bodily power to preach. While transcending women relied upon the Holy Spirit's power to authorize their preaching, the transgressing women found power in breaking social rules. While the virtuous women drew strength—as well as a prescription for behavior—from a culturally approved female presentation, women who modeled male forms drew from bodies already legitimized to preach. To read the history of female preaching as a bodily history is to take seriously the choices women made related to their physicality. It is to acknowledge the limits of those choices, limitations emerging most often through society's reactions. Ultimately, it is to understand preaching as a deeply embodied practice.

A history of female preachers' habitations provides greater tools for grasping the multiple ways women have navigated their bodies as they have preached. It tells us something of how such habits evolved, and in their actions we can recognize our own. Thinking about women who attempted to escape their femaleness, contemporary preachers examine their own complex relationship to being female and preacher. Thinking about the various embodiments of virtue prompts considerations around how society still shapes our conceptions of being a woman or our definitions of appropriate attire for preaching. At the center of all these choices is the persistent reality that a female body can be controversial in the pulpit. All four habitations "flesh out" the discomfort with being female in the pulpit.[81] They demonstrate how women responded to larger conversations about purity, sacred space, physicality, proclamation, and femininity. Discomfort with female preachers' bodies continues, evidenced in present-day women who suggest they have to leave their bodies to preach, view their bodies as a distraction to preaching, or name how they can feel exposed in the pulpit. Others also notice this discomfort. In his introductory remarks to Lee McGee's *Wrestling with the Patriarchs*, Thomas Troeger notes the difficulty he has witnessed among female preaching students, as well as the high degree of intensity and complexity embedded within those struggles.[82]

The complexity of the struggle—as well the complexity within the habitations—cautions against set conclusions about the preacher's best uses of her body. Transgressing social conventions about female forms is not necessarily a more powerful mode of communication than preaching as a virtuous woman, even though it may have resulted in greater publicity. It might not even, in the final analysis, be more truly resistant to dominant norms. A woman who stresses the power of the Holy Spirit while minimizing her body may discover that she is preaching with more bodily presence than she first believed. There is no one, grand, overarching habitation for female preaching. Nor, by any means, do these four bundles of

81. I am indebted to Rowan Williams for the term "fleshed out."
82. McGee, *Wrestling with the Patriarchs*, 9.

habitations provide a complete account of the possible preaching habits. No one preacher fits exclusively into one set of habitations. Jemima Wilkinson named herself the Universal Public Friend while making use of male forms. Catherine Booth adhered to virtuous practices, but her support of the Hallelujah Lasses and her assertion that women possess the natural abilities to preach hinted toward a more nuanced understanding of femaleness in preaching. Elder Lucy Smith combined a variety of forms, borrowing the dress styles of virtuous women but keeping her hair in a cropped cut, relying upon male-associated strengths like administrative skill while being called "Mother" by her majority female-membered church. The preachers named in this overview drew more heavily upon one set of habitations while continually reaching into other sets. Rev. Lewis's embodiments also utilized multiple habitations in paradoxical, complex ways. Her simple attire, her belief in the body's role to support but not overtake her words, and her willingness to experiment with dance coalesce into a performance that shows traces of each habitation. Taken all together, Rev. Lewis extends the models, a reminder that every preaching body is far more than a type.

Perhaps what is most telling, though, is Rev. Lewis's initial lack of words for grasping the meaning-making efforts contained within her embodied life. While articulating a theology of preaching with ease and having thoughtfully described the factors contributing to her bodily decisions, she grew quiet when asked about a theology of the body. "This is a good question," she said. If a bodily history of female preaching holds significance beyond a set of interesting descriptions, its significance lies in its power to unearth the breach that lies between embodied existence and one's preaching life.[83] Stepping into a space in which her body carries a host of assumptions, meanings, and symbolic power, a female preacher can experience bodily discomfort without much explanatory power about its history or enough resources to dispel its powerful grip. When our habitations are "magical," as Merleau-Ponty suggests, we don't think about what we are doing and why we are doing it. When we become uneasy in the disjunctions between our movements and our world, we start to examine our habitations and, at times, allow our habits to be retooled. We might copy the preaching habits of colleagues, discovering our adjusted embodied presence receives greater reception even as it feels unfamiliar to us. If

---

83. Rowan Williams suggests that not only is "history a set of stories we tell in order to understand who we are and the world we're now in," but history also is written "to organize the collective memory so that breaches may be mended and identities displayed" (*Why Study the Past?*, 1, 5).

we have the time and resources, we might study a variety of preaching embodiments, comparing other habitations to our own and continuing to experiment. With habitations shaped by history, communities, and the body's material specificity, a female preacher possesses a host of connections and breaches, some that she may be able to clearly articulate and some that prove more difficult to unpack.

A history of the body's habitations uncovers some of the unnamed assumptions or unreflective behaviors that can accompany female preaching. In so doing, the history provides tools for intentionality.[84] The woman who is aware of her body's place in a long line of history becomes self-conscious about the habits within her preaching. She is better equipped to make choices about her body's presentation and movements and more able to consider the significance of her choices. Women make daily decisions about their bodies and their preaching. There is the preacher who chooses to wear cowboy boots instead of her typical pumps, the one who debates about painted fingernails or hoop earrings in the pulpit, and the one who tries to stop tilting her head in ways that have drawn congregational criticism. With a sense of the historical streams in which her body stands, the female preacher can examine how she inhabits her preaching world. She can reflect on her choices, noting the habits she has inherited and the norms in which she lives. She can find ways to affirm, as Rev. Lewis eventually articulated, "Our bodies are God's vehicles through which we serve. God gave me this body to be used as an instrument." Using these historical yet malleable tools, she can analyze her weekly preaching decisions, thinking about the meaning of her agency in her efforts to embody God's word. With this bodily history of female preaching in place, the present-day preachers' embodied choices now take center stage.

84. Smith writes, "In telling a history of what we take for granted, a generic history lifts up for critical consideration some assumptions we use without thinking about them" ("Practical History of Preaching," 7).

CHAPTER 3

My Clothes Teach and Preach

On Pentecost Sunday in a Gothic-style church bursting with people, a woman stood up to preach. The Reverend Caroline Walker was a self-assured, welcoming figure, with captivating eyes and expressive hands. She possessed an understated yet definite presence in the pulpit. Rev. Walker's clothing reflected the day's festive spirit. Over a cream-colored alb, she wore a red silk chasuble with a dove and flames painted across the front. The color filled the space just as her body did, visually bearing the fiery passion of Pentecost to her congregation. Rev. Walker's Pentecost chasuble was one among many in her wardrobe. Her congregation had grown accustomed to the green and gold one that accompanied them through the summer. They favored the blue one that returned each Advent. By her attire, Rev. Walker guided her congregation through the Christian liturgical year. Her vestments played a role in creating her priestly presence among them.

"What I wear is a big part of the preaching task for me," said Rev. Walker. "I am and have been for a while a pastor of traditional black churches and within that milieu there is still an expectation that the pastor will look good." She veered away from the black pulpit robe of her predecessors, because the alb is "the more normative garb for today." She purchased albs specifically tailored for her physical frame, ensuring her dress followed her womanly curves. Her chasubles symbolized what she called the Anglo-Catholic roots of her congregation; an aspect of Wesleyan heritage she believed was often overlooked within the worshiping life of black Methodists. Combining a respect for her congregation's expectations, a desire to acknowledge her femaleness, and an aim to teach a "whole new body of symbology" around the Christian liturgical year, Rev. Walker invested time, money, and effort into her Sunday morning wardrobe. She viewed clothing as artful communication. "I am a person who loves color and for me, fashion is . . . an expression. I would never just get up [and] pull down that oatmeal alb out of the closet," she said emphatically. "So my clothes preach. And teach. And for me as a woman and as a woman who loves apparel as art that is an important statement."

On another Sunday in a different town, the Reverend Erin Robinson wore decidedly different preaching attire. Serving an inner-city congregation that eschews robes, she chose not to push her preference for wearing an alb. Instead, she adopted a relaxed version of the pantsuit, dressing her tall frame in blue, tailored slacks, a white shirt and a loosely cut, light blue jacket with embroidered trim. To this ensemble she added a stole, color coordinated with her clothes or connected to the morning's worship theme. Her decisions around clothes were based upon two criteria: minimizing the attention directed toward her appearance while simultaneously projecting a professional look. "I want," she said, "to dress in a way that takes my appearance off the table. I aim to dress so perfectly appropriately that no one notices what I'm wearing." While Rev. Walker sought to draw attention to her clothes, Rev. Robinson sought to deflect it. "I like to dress the way I like to dress," she continued. "But I try to dress appropriately. My overall philosophy is if I dress perfectly, then the way I look becomes a nonissue." Like Rev. Walker, Rev. Robinson communicated through her clothes. But rather than teach a "whole new symbology," she aimed for inconspicuous perfection, believing the flawless outfit bolstered her professional respectability.

Both women's choices were the result of careful deliberation, a thinking through of the female body in the pulpit and the body's role while preaching. Clothes are a mode of embodiment.[1] They express something of how we inhabit the world. Dressing for the same task, the two preachers made divergent choices. One woman wore clothes that taught her congregation about the liturgical calendar and emphasized her priestly authority. She intentionally drew attention to her body. Another woman hoped her clothing choices would not be noticed by the congregation. With equal forethought, she sought clothes that deflected attention away from her body. The meaning each preacher attached to her choice reveals a delicate

---

1. Weber and Mitchell write, "Clothes wear bodies. Dresses express extensions and connections to the body and are themselves a mode of embodiment" (*Not Just Any Dress*, 261–62).

balance between bodily potential and peril. The preacher's clothing could participate in the proclamation or, if wrongly chosen, hinder it. If artfully expressive clothes stood as a glorious ideal, then the potential for clothes to distract served as a restraining reality.

Choosing Clothes to Preach

The question "What should I wear?" is a universal one. "Dressing is a part of our everyday presentation of self, a statement we make consciously or unconsciously as we go about living our lives."[2] Every person, male or female, chooses clothes daily. Such choices communicate our fashion preferences, social class, and daily work.[3] When women pondered clothing for preaching, these influences were joined by other factors, including dress requirements for sacred space and the public nature of their role. Expectations abounded, flowing from the mores of their tradition, the standards around professional attire, and the preferences of a congregation. Deliberating amid these variables, this small group of women made diverse choices in clothes for preaching and drew diverse meanings about their decisions.

Rev. Walker's colorful vestments were an aspect of her personality, an extension of her style, put to use as a liturgical tool. Rabbi Julie Kahn wore the standard black preaching gown to which her congregation was accustomed, which both covered her body and linked her to past, male preachers. She disliked its bulky nature but relished the way it marked her role. Rev. Robinson chose a suit, aiming for non-distracting dress through a widely accepted workplace uniform tailored to her style. Rev. Joan Anderson recently began wearing pants when preaching, violating a long-standing personal taboo barring pants on women in worship. She appreciated the increased mobility, but found even greater delight in donning once forbidden clothes. Clothes did teach and preach; offering a window into the specific ways each woman embodied her task.

This chapter will attempt a lived body analysis of preachers' clothing decisions. It will reflect upon a woman's given physicality, surrounding

2. Ibid., 261.

3. Weber and Mitchell continue, "Although we may not be immediately aware of it, talking about clothes forces us to speak, directly or indirectly, about our bodies, about details of material culture, about context, about commerce and commodification, about social expectations and personal aspirations, about media influence, family relationships, work, play, values, social structure and more" (ibid., 4).

culture, which included her theological tradition, and the agential spark that enabled her "freedom" of choice amid her "facts."[4] The preachers of this study developed clothing habitations from a series of commonly shared, foundational structures. Rev. Walker's assertion that "clothes preach and teach" foreshadowed theological considerations accompanying worship leaders. Rev. Robinson's stance that "clothes should not distract" acknowledged the historical contentiousness of female bodies, as well as standards of professional dress. The women of this study articulated how dress choices balanced the multiple embodiments of preacher, professional, and female.

Historically, female preachers managed being female and preacher through clothing choices designed to increase the body's acceptability. The habitations of looking virtuous, borrowing male-associated articles of clothing, downplaying the body, or accentuating it in boundary-breaking ways influenced the women in this study. Rather than single personas to be wholly adopted, these habitations wove themselves in and out of their decisions. Rev. Robinson's blue slacks and white shirt hinted toward male-like clothing. Her more pastel jacket leaned toward a virtuous female, while her stated aim was to downplay her body's role in preaching. Rev. Walker's bright, decorative vestments, which were unusual for her tradition and unusually prominent from the pulpit, played the role of transgressing boundaries while simultaneously representing some of the oldest garments worn by preachers across history. These threads could be mixed and matched, drawn from or set aside, and even pulled out as well-worn tropes when advantageous, but rarely whole-heartedly adopted in ways documented in other eras. Instead they were relied upon when needed to enable a fresh and individualized embodiment of preacher, professional, and female.

By continually balancing the norms of looking clerical and professional along with being female, the women's choices made manifest Mahmood's conception of agency. Mahmood argues that agency happens in the multiple ways women inhabit existing structures of subordination.[5] Subordination, in this context, is understood as those structures of governance that call subjects into being.[6] Clerical and professional dress operated with governing structures. Certain clothes signified each identity. Put another way, there are standards of dress that constituted a clergy person and the

---

4. I am returning to Young's assertion that agency happens at the intersection of facticity and freedom.

5. Mahmood, "Agency," 180.

6. See Butler, *Psychic Life of Power*, 3–11.

professional class. Being female also involved a certain dress code, a fluid one that has changed across history and context but nevertheless still casts its influence. Entering into the expectations embedded in these three roles, women made choices about their preaching clothes. As such, their seemingly straightforward decisions about what to wear contained meaning-laden insights into the modes of existence within which these women lived and preached.

The complex dilemma of navigating three sets of standards remained inherent in all clothing decisions. However, the specific range of choices women faced was shaped by their religious traditions. In broad strokes, women preached either in settings that expected prescribed clerical attire or in settings that did not require such garments. This chapter will explore both scenarios, delving first into the experiences of women who wore what is formally defined as clerical dress.

Dressing in Clergy-Prescribed Clothes

The almost Reverend Melissa Clark did not wear a robe while preaching. Serving as an intern at a church with a more informal worship style, she encountered a senior pastor who held firm rules around non-ordained, seminary students wearing vestments reserved for clergy. But Ms. Clark had worn an alb in other settings. Reminiscing about that experience and thinking ahead to her ordination, she said, "If I could wear a robe, I would wear a robe. I used to wear albs when I served communion in college. And I loved putting on my alb. It made me look at the people differently. It made me really aware of what I was doing. And it is ancient."

In confessing her desire for a preaching robe, Ms. Clark articulated a preference for dress that linked her to history and sharpened her readiness for her role. Her nascent explanation hinted at the authority derived from wearing albs, robes, or gowns for preaching. Of the women represented in this story, a large majority of them chose garments that had been marked for use by clergy during worship. While denominational practices or congregational expectations factored into their choices, the benefits gained from such clothes were identified easily. Women named how ecclesial clothes heightened their visual presence, granted authority, and provided a cover for their bodies. "I loved putting on my alb," Ms. Clark reminisced. That affinity resounded across the preachers, as they experienced an alb teaching a congregation and themselves about their preaching role. "While I might change my shoes Sunday to Sunday," said Rev. Lewis, "the robe stays on."

Albs, cassocks, robes, and preaching gowns all have a history in Christian worship. Their basic form can be traced to the everyday dress of ancient Rome.[7] The early church gravitated toward the "humble tunics of the servant class" for both clergy and laity.[8] The plain, flowing gowns, typically white or flax in color, evolved into attire specifically designated for worship leadership between the fifth and sixth centuries.[9] As worship practices developed, other elements, including color, ornamental designs, and decorative layers, were incorporated into the once simple gowns. Alternate styles of dress also emerged. Cassocks derived from albs, first as an additional outer coat and then as its own, separate dress.[10] The cassocks of ordinary clergy were black, adding to white a second ecclesial color. During the Protestant Reformation, the Geneva gown, or pulpit robe, was introduced. The gown was a black, freely flowing robe similar in style to academic or American judicial attire.[11] Five hundred years later, the original *tunica alb* reemerged during the liturgical renewal movement of the twentieth century in a form that echoed its earlier style.[12] Although slightly different from one another, robes, cassocks, and albs share the common characteristics of being basic in form, comprised of black or white material, and readily identifiable as the authorized clothes of church or synagogue.[13] Wearing them created a line between secular and sacred, and between congregation and chancel, pulpit or bema. When putting on her robe, Rev. Anderson remarked, "I do like to feel pastoral. I do like to feel like I am clergy."

The women of this study who wore robes, albs, or preaching gowns noticed how the attire visually signified their roles, making them publicly

7. Mayo, *History of Ecclesiastical Dress*, 11. See also Chrysostomos, *Orthodox Liturgical Dress*, 20.

8. Rubinstein writes, "The Christian sects that hid in the catacombs in Rome took on the humble tunics of the servant class. These 'servants of the Lord' replaced the toga with a symbol of asceticism" (*Dress Codes*, 90).

9. Down traces how clergy "held on to the traditional 'civilized' dress" of ancient Rome during the descent into the Dark Ages. This dress became "the distinctive and peculiar robes of the clergy . . . [and] served to distinguish clergy from the laity throughout the Middle Ages" ("Costume of the Clergy," 349).

10. Mayo, *History of Ecclesiastical Dress*, 40; Macalister, *Ecclesiastical Vestments*, 194.

11. Macalister, *Ecclesiastical Vestments*, 207.

12. Mayo, *History of Ecclesiastical Dress*, 31.

13. Ibid., 15–19.

recognizable and personally aware of their responsibilities. "I wear a garment that symbolizes pastoral authority and symbolizes faith," remarked Rev. Harris. Rabbi Monica Levin said, "When I put on a kippa it allows me to be a different person in some ways. It gives credibility to whatever it is we are going to say or do. It marks the moment as different. It allows me to be the figure, Rabbi Monica." By heightening these preachers' physical presence and sense of sacred responsibility, these garments enabled the body to be marked as a liturgical leader. These women put on the clothes long associated with preaching and then took up preaching.

The authorizing power of a robe or alb derives, in part, from its function as a uniform. A uniform works to "designate membership in a group."[14] It affirms the wearer has mastered the necessary skills and an outside authority has granted membership status.[15] The women who wore liturgical garments for preaching articulated the ways such attire functioned as a uniform. They appreciated the ability to be a blank slate, with the accompanying depersonalization of their particular bodies. This quality was especially valued in moments when a woman experienced a congregation's questioning of her legitimacy. Serving a church while in seminary, Rev. Baker articulated how her alb provided additional credibility for herself and her congregation. She reported, "I came into a much older congregation, where there were a lot of men. I'm young and I'm a student. The alb gave me an air of authority. It gave me a presence." External recognition bolstered her internal confidence. She added, "The alb helps me focus. It really does." Rev. Harris also experienced the power of a uniform. Wearing her white alb during the early weeks of a new pastorate, she received numerous comments from congregants that they could not hear her voice. Acting on the advice of a colleague, she switched one Sunday to a black preaching robe. The robe's darker color contrasted well with the white walls of the sanctuary. It also matched the attire of previous male senior pastors. The complaints about not being able to hear her voice ceased. In this instance, the right uniform provided an entry into all manner of recognition and acceptance.

In addition to casting preacherly authority, liturgically prescribed clothes offered the advantage of covering the body. The women in this study spoke of the freedom they gained and the confidence they experienced knowing a long, flowing garment obscured their breasts, hips, and legs, thereby minimizing their femininity. When discussing such gowns,

14. Rubinstein, *Dress Codes*, 86.
15. Ibid.

they routinely employed terms like "de-gendered," "gender neutral," or "androgynous" to describe their appearance. Rev. Baker said, "Once the robe goes on, it is more asexual. I am who I am and I can't take being female out of the equation. But I think the robe neutralizes it a lot." In addition, these garments hid their street clothes. "I prefer to wear a robe," said Rev. Harris, "I just feel more comfortable in it because I'm not worried about what I am wearing." Rev. Baker agreed. "My alb helps me not worry," she said. "It allows me to be free and expressive." One Sunday she inadvertently left her robe at home. She felt decidedly uncomfortable leading worship. "I had worn a sleeveless dress sweater with a high turtleneck collar," she remembered. Worrying about whether her arms looked exposed while she preached, she said, "was like being naked in the pulpit."

Even amid their appreciation for the gender-minimizing features of a robe, women injected elements of femininity into the prescribed clothes. Most often, they added color to their clothes. Rev. Harris frequently wore a lavender stole, whose soft color and weaving grapevines evoked a more feminine look. Rabbi Kahn chose pink or white beaded kippot rather than the black yarmulkes worn by her male colleagues. Seeking more variety in her preaching attire, Rev. Anderson consecrated an African dress to expand her traditional wardrobe for leading worship. She explained, "I wanted something different. I wanted something that was feminine because most of the robes were plain. So I was in an African store and they had these dresses. It was a beautiful sapphire robe trimmed in silver. I've never worn it outside of [worship]." Keeping the covering power of a robe, women created smaller, less risky ways to represent their female selves.

Liturgically prescribed clothes were not the only set of uniforms operating within this group of female preachers. Clothing expectations—and the language of a uniform—carried over into decisions about other clothes. Women navigated another set of standards as they preached in spaces that did not require ecclesial dress. Here the clothes taken straight from their home closets became the preacher's outfit for the day.

A Second Layer: Discerning Professional Dress

Existing alongside the women who wear albs, cassocks, and robes were the women who preached without distinctive clerical gowns. Three women in the study preached regularly in what might be termed lay attire or street clothes. Several other preachers laid aside their gowns when preaching in certain settings or occasions. And most preachers, knowing that their lay clothes were displayed before and after worship, pondered these choices with care. They asked such questions as "What are the congregation's expectations around my dress?" "What image do I want to convey?" and "What clothes are most comfortable to me?" As with more liturgically identified clothes, women weighed external expectations alongside stylistic preferences. Clothing norms shifted in this category, with less attention directed toward a particular ecclesial look and more focus upon the standards of professional dress.

While their wardrobe expanded, so did their concerns about distracting dress. Describing her guidelines for preaching attire, Rev. Erica Williams said, "Because I am a relatively young person, I'm very aware of not having my body be a physical distraction to others, young males especially. I definitely try to make sure nothing is revealing or too tight. I'm particularly conscious of my chest not looking really exposed or busty." Elaborating on why she labored to select the right outfit, Rev. Anderson reflected, "I wear something that is pleasing to the eye but will not raise questions about what I'm trying to portray." Without the cover of a long gown, women considered the riskiness of their attire diverting attention or hindering their role. Without the sacred associations of liturgically prescribed clothes, their clothes took on a theological role.

"Ordinary" clothes did contain liturgical dimensions. They may not have possessed ecclesial meaning derived from history or a liturgical calendar. Yet they conveyed an alternate but no less theologically vital message about the equality existing between clergy and laity.[16] Some Christian traditions, as well as some specific congregations, emphasize the necessity of preachers wearing everyday clothes to visually represent the continuous line stretching between pulpit and pew. Rev. Robinson's attire represented her sensitivity to her specific context. She explained, "In my context, we have a lot of people who struggle with Christianity. So I didn't really push the robe thing. There are some very anti-clerical folks." The women in this study who preached regularly in lay attire worked in congregations that promoted shared commonalities between pulpit and pew. While some might have preferred to preach in a robe, they chose the clothes that best matched their community's desires and practices. In so doing, they recognized that

---

16. While looking precisely at the Reformation, Down notes, "At different times in history, clergy lay aside distinctive dress in favor of looking 'just like everyone else'" ("Costume of the Clergy," 350).

each clothing choice brought a message, just as they pondered precisely what clothes—and what message—they wanted to convey.

Without a dividing line between clergy and lay dress, their deliberations brought to the forefront the influence of culture upon dress. Rather than a gown that conveys a host of religious symbols, the preachers chose clothes that signified the skilled character of their position. Their dress deliberations blended the multiple criteria used to define professional dress: the expectations of the workplace, the historical habitations formed around female preacher's clothes, and the styles popular within contemporary fashion. The monochrome grey suit, the mix-and-match skirt and jacket, the sheath dress, and the Ann Taylor pants with a sweater set were all represented within this group. As they balanced social guidelines, they also carefully investigated their congregations, noticing the standards operating in their localized places. Women understood the importance of fulfilling all these expectations, just as they encountered moments when they stretched the norms.

When Rabbi Kahn began serving at a new congregation, one of the leaders initiated a conversation about her dress. "She said," recalled Rabbi Kahn, "if you want the possibility of optimal success, dress in a skirt suit every day, for a while, so that congregants won't judge you on what you are wearing but on what you say and do as a rabbi.'" Rabbi Kahn followed her advice, wearing skirt suits, heels, and stockings throughout the long, hot days of summer. "Around November," she continued, "It was getting cold. I was doing funerals and my legs were getting cold. I started wearing pantsuits every day." Rabbi Kahn maintained the suit standard for several years. "Last year," she said "was the first year when I started wearing slacks and a sweater on days when I don't have a lot going on." Then she ended, almost as an afterthought, "Of course, when preaching on the bema I wear skirts. We would never wear pants on the bema."

The classic suit first appeared over two hundred years ago, and its form remains almost unaltered today.[17] Designed for men, the suit outlined the body's form without adhering too closely to it.[18] It clothed the body from neck to ankle, typically in dark colors. Worn throughout the ensuing centuries, the suit has evolved into the "standard costume of civil leadership for the whole world" and the universally accepted business uniform.[19] A host

17. Hollander, *Sex and Suits*, 4.

18. Ibid., 54.

19. Ibid., 55.

of semiotic terms are associated with suits, including diplomacy, restraint, detachment, and confidence.[20] The suit, as one scholar asserts "indicated that, so attired, the individual will . . . conduct himself or herself in the expected 'professional' manner."[21] When women entered the workforce in large numbers during the last decades of the twentieth century, they took up the existing male suit. They gained credibility through clothes historically linked to status and power, substituting a skirt for slacks in order to fulfill the dress expectations of their gender.[22] In the late 1980s, when the first females were approved for ordination in the Evangelical Church of Finland, they were given an official outfit: a black skirt suit with gray pinstripes and a white, high-collared shirt.[23] The standard endures. "When I think preaching," said Ms. Clark, "I think suit."

Years after that first-week-on-the-job conversation, Rabbi Kahn remembered the instruction she received with clarity. A suit minimized the attention directed to her clothing choices. The reasoning behind the attire matched the rationale Rev. Robinson gave for her clothing choices, illustrating the belief that clothes communicate about the wearer and acknowledging that a cost exists for those who choose incorrectly. A suit, historically associated with membership in a profession, confers credibility upon the female preacher. It functions as a uniform, providing authority similar to an alb or robe. Even when her wardrobe choices relaxed into shirts and slacks, Rabbi Kahn held to skirt suits for preaching days, that fail-safe option to take her appearance off the table.

Other preachers also reflected a journey from suits to more relaxed attire. This transition happened over time, as their gains in experience increased their confidence and strengthened their pastoral identity. Wearing a suit, or exclusively wearing suits, was replaced with a variety of clothing options that still maintained the designation as "professional attire." Precisely what constituted professional, though, varied from preacher to preacher.

As one who preached regularly without clerical attire, Rev. Williams typically chose dark-colored pants and a blouse. She noted how she "wore far more suits in the beginning months" before gravitating to shirts and slacks. Working in a rural church, Rev. Williams's attire was more formal than the

20. Ibid., 113.

21. Rubinstein, *Dress Codes*, 86.

22. Ibid., 115.

23. Stjerna, "What Will They Wear?," 44.

secretary's jeans and polo shirt. It was professional for her context. Situated in a rapidly growing outer suburb, Rabbi Levin wore suits in the early years of her ministry. Then she became pregnant. Her clothes shifted to maternity dresses, shirts and skirts, blouses and slacks. After giving birth, she did not return to wearing suits, instead continuing to mix her styles. Reflecting on her decisions, she said, "There have been times that I've rebelled. The suit is too formal or too distant. I like to feel when I come to service that I'm being a part of the family. This is my sixth year here. I do wear a dress once in a while. It is not such a big deal. I still look professional." Time, history, and a changing body expanded the array of her choices and her definition of appropriate dress. The norm of professional held, even as the boundaries around its definition became more fluid. Rev. Harris detailed a similar journey toward less formal clothes. She said, "I worry [about clothes] a lot less than I used to." After acquiring several years of ministerial experience, she intentionally began selecting less formal clothes, wearing sweaters with skirts of various lengths, ruffled blouses and slacks, and even t-shirts and jeans. She dressed, she said, to "promote a slightly more casual atmosphere in the church." She elaborated, "When I first came [to this congregation], it was really formal. Dress is one way of conveying that . . . it is okay to come in your jeans." Rev. Harris's relaxed clothing choices landed on the edges of professional dress. She altered her clothes over time, perceiving them to be an aspect of her pastoral leadership. Her attire was a method of preaching and teaching in the same manner as Rev. Walker's fiery Pentecost chasuble.

It is easy to understand why women gravitated to suits and other forms of professional dress. Donning these clothes sent a message about a preacher's readiness for her task, her capacity to competently deliver a sermon. Just as liturgically prescribed clothes conveyed membership status in the ecclesial body of those authorized to preach, professional attire provided a layer of legitimacy to the preacher. Clothes served as a tool to affirm their credentialed identity, enabling them to embody the preaching role.

The category of professional dress, while always encompassing the suit, proved to be a diverse and localized one. What constituted professional varied from preacher to preacher, depending upon context and personhood. As her role became embodied in a preacher, her clothing choices reflected a growing internal authority. Rev. Harris's jeans gained her credibility as the leader of an "everyone is welcome" congregation. Rabbi Levin's dress projected bonds of kinship where the preacher is a member of the family. Without using words, these particular embodiments were teaching tools, offering a message about the wide range of acceptable preaching bodies.

What is harder to discern from these short snapshots is precisely how critical clothing choices were to establishing membership or legitimacy. Clothes are important. Choosing wrongly might hinder a preacher. But when discussing their clothes, these women reported more anxiety about the possibility of selecting an outfit deemed inappropriate than actual instances of wearing such an outfit and being judged accordingly. Rev. Robinson's statement, "I aim to dress so perfectly appropriate that no one notices what I am wearing," revealed an abiding awareness of the potential to distract inherent in their bodies, as well as the reality that a congregation could—and did—observe their choices.

The Preacher in Pants

Amid the shifting boundaries of professional dress, Rabbi Kahn held to the standard of a skirt for preaching days. Even if she wore other outfits during the week, she wore a skirt when on the bema. The skirt standard could be attributed to historical forms of female dress or the expectations for formal clothes in worship. For Rabbi Kahn, and other women, the skirt appeared to symbolize the perfectly perfect attire. It was the outfit deemed most immune from being labeled a distraction.

Rev. Anderson also grew up with a similar standard for worship. She remembered, "We were taught to wear skirts. When I started [preaching] twenty-five years ago, women didn't wear pants to church." Then she inadvertently pulled a muscle in her neck, which ignited an old injury. In the ensuing months, her body lacked its normal flexibility. "One [Sunday] morning, I couldn't bend to put on stockings," she remembered. So she wore pants to church. "I was very uncomfortable," she said, but no one noticed. As her recovery continued, she continued to wear pants, without any comments or criticism from her congregation. She continued, "I had to totally transition in my mind because I was accustomed to wearing skirts and stockings. It was a slow transition, but now I love wearing pants." When asked to elaborate on her preference, Rev. Anderson cited the increased mobility and comfort she experienced in slacks. "I felt liberated," she concluded.

Rev. Anderson was not the only woman to preach regularly in pants. Ms. Clark remarked, "When I first started preaching, I would never wear pants. In the past year, I have overcome that hurdle. Now I wear dress slacks to preach." The two other women who preached in street clothes often chose pants. Several women preferred pants beneath their robes. Rev. Lewis was one of those women and, like Rev. Anderson, any initial discomfort and worry about congregational disapproval faded over time. Within this small group, wearing pants while preaching was a regular occurrence. Pants were chosen for comfort, covering, and ease of movement. Each of these factors contained an element of liberation, a release from discomfort, exposure, and constraint. Yet the material benefits found in pants might not adequately capture the sense of freedom Rev. Anderson articulated. Her journey included casting aside inherited restrictions about women's dress in sacred space. Altering her attire in response to her body's needs, her words—I felt liberated—seemed to indicate a more embodied presence.

When detailing the historical distinctions between male and female dress in Western European societies, some scholars trace a legacy of corporeal concealment in female clothes.[24] While male fashion styles, from plates of armor to the first suits, followed the body's contours and accurately represent its form, female styles worked to conceal, confuse, or obscure female physicality through skirts that hid the body below the waist and bodices or shirts that reshaped the chest.[25] Anne Hollander asserts that men's fashion styles held to "a formal authenticity derived from human corporeal facts" that was absent in female clothes.[26] Only in the past century have clothing designs begun to adhere to actual female proportions, bringing the female body more into focus alongside shifts in women's access to education, work outside the home, and the right to vote.[27]

Pants, in addition to being archetypal male dress, are clothes that follow the body's form.[28] Pants enable one's corporeal facts—one's physicality—to be authentically represented. It is this authenticity, or real representation,

24. Rubinstein, *Dress Codes*, 119.

25. Hollander writes, "Male fashion is based on the brilliant bodily articulations of plate armor, while female fashion exaggerates the enveloping skirt below with a small tight bodice above" (*Sex and Suits*, 35).

26. Hollander asserts, "The design of male dress has a foundation in the structure of the whole physical body, a formal authenticity derived from human corporeal facts" (ibid., 48).

27. Ibid., 147–48.

28. Rubinstein, *Dress Codes*, 12.

that is key to grasping why preaching in pants could be liberating to some women. If one is preaching in clothes that hide the body or obscure it or alter it from what it actually is, then one may experience a disconnection between bodily life and sermon. If one feels obligated to preach in clothes that change the body to fit a feminine ideal, then one's preaching may feel less embodied. Pants provide one possible platform for corporeal facts, potentially strengthening the tie between embodied self and proclamation.[29]

To Teach, to Preach, and to Potentially Distract

When examining the clothing choices of these preachers, their decisions appear straightforward. Women wore either clerical gowns or "lay" professional dress. They adhered to social expectations and ecclesial standards. With a few exceptions, they made only slight adjustments to uniform clothes, maintaining the established norms of contemporary preacher attire. Their choices appear recognizable, predictable, and able to be classified without delving too deeply.

Yet such quick categorization belies the enormous weight of historical, cultural, theological, ecclesial, and personal expectations. The weight is revealed in the evocative phrases scattered throughout the chapter: "the pastor will look good," "my clothes preach and teach," "an alb is ancient," and "dress for optimal success." Women experienced their clothing decisions as a foundational, vital element of their preaching embodiments and a means by which they affirmed their preaching identity. Rev. Walker summed up her reflections by stating, "I believe the body is a gift. How I dress is a reflection not just of myself but of the Creator."

Every embodiment contains and creates meaning. Building upon the idea that clothes preach, women discovered their clothes to be tools in their proclamation, teaching theology and ecclesiology, liturgical time and pastoral presence. With clothes serving as a mode of embodiment, their attire was a building block in their preaching bodies. Clothes could help authorize them as preachers, affirming that space was available for a female preaching body. When discussing the Finnish female priests' suits, Stjerna concluded,

29. Hollander argues for the necessity of clothes that reveal rather than conceal women's legs. She writes, "Demonstrating women's full humanity was essential; and that meant showing that they had bodies not unlike men's in many particulars. To show that women have ordinary working legs . . . was also to show that they have ordinary working muscles and tendons, as well as spleen and livers, lungs and stomachs, and by extension, brains" (*Sex and Suits*, 61–62).

"We first women pastors had our brief career as fashion-model-teaching-theologians. Teaching people new symbols, helping them to associate their understandings and experiences of ministry and church with something so very new: women pastors, an impossibility that was becoming real in front of their eyes."[30] Each body that preaches also teaches about the diversity of bodies able to preach.

On the other hand, the opportunity to teach through their attire always lived in tension with the potential to distract. The risk of dress that diverts attention from the sermon was an ever-present concern. "How you present yourself is very important," said Rabbi Levin. "I don't want to draw away. I don't want to be distracting." While any person could wear attire that detracted from their message, these women framed the issue of distracting dress as rooted in their gender. When narrating her aim to render her appearance a nonissue, Rev. Robinson concluded, "The standard for me as a female preacher is a level of perfection in dress that allows everyone to forget that I am female." The real distraction appeared to be the femaleness of the body beneath the clothes. Hence the robe that fully hid the body became a means by which to feel free and an unexpected occasion of preaching without a gown's cover felt like "being naked in the pulpit."

As Mahmood so aptly asserts, the meaning embedded in choices never can be determined outside of an analysis of "the particular concepts that enabled specific modes of being."[31] Only in recent history have women received official permission to preach. For centuries this mode of being was not available to them by virtue of their female bodies. One could not be a woman and a preacher. If women are moving into a new space, a new mode of being, then it makes sense that they carry within themselves an enduring anxiety about being female—or too female—in the pulpit. Hence they chose clothes that covered their bodies, minimized their feminine features, or injected femininity in small, socially sanctioned ways such as a splash of color or a suit skirt. The basic dilemma of preaching as her fully embodied, female self remained. Further exploration of this dilemma involves the next layer of dress decisions. Here women added more explicit markers of femininity to their basic attire through adornments or accessories.

30. Stjerna, "What Will They Wear?," 45.
31. Mahmood, "Agency," 186.

CHAPTER 4

Looking Like Me:
Self-Expression through Adornments

The Reverend Joan Anderson experienced a call to ministry amid a multitude of male clergy and a strict dress code for preachers. "We were taught to wear black and white," she said. A black suit with a white shirt was the expected attire for clergy. Disliking a look she equated with being "just one of the guys," Rev. Anderson consciously worked to appear more feminine. While many female colleagues still wore a black suit with a white, high-collared blouse, she chose her attire, which varied from suits to shirts and skirts to dresses, from a rainbow of colors. She added to her ensemble light makeup, jewelry, and heeled shoes. She intentionally fashioned her hair in what she termed a feminine style, maintaining a layered, flowing cut. When asked why she deviated from the norms of her tradition, she stated, "I don't think God called me to be like men. I believe God called me to be who I am." A part of who she is is female.

Rev. Rebecca Harris followed the dress code of her church, wearing an alb and stole each Sunday. But she consciously picked her shoes in response to the alb's androgynous feel. "I like to wear feminine shoes," she said. "I am a woman, that is part of who I am, and God created me this way." Like Rev. Anderson, Rev. Harris incorporated her female identity into at least one aspect of her physical presentation. Rev. Walker echoed the same sentiment when she commented, "It is important to me that the way I dress reflects the fact that I am a woman." Their voices were joined by the reflections of Rev. Deborah Lewis. Although she did not touch explicitly upon femininity in her style, her words held the aim for self-expression. "I'm not one of those people who felt called to ministry at twelve years old," she said. "I've watched many different role models and I don't aim for a persona. I'm very comfortable in my own skin." Each time she detailed her jewelry, makeup, or hair, she concluded by stating, "I'm just me. I'm very much me."

The Inclination toward Female Presentations

When deciding how to present their bodies for preaching, women weighed two coexisting aspirations. They sought to look like preachers, making decisions about their basic ensemble based upon prevailing ecclesial and professional standards. But alongside those criteria, they held an accompanying desire to look like themselves, to appear as the women God created them to be. Professional and clerical sensibilities had dominated the decisions between robes or suits, cassocks or tailored shirts and slacks. The second desire for self-expression might appear through slight variations or additions to the uniform dress. The impulse gained momentum as the realm of women's choices moved from their basic outfit to the adorning elements of their appearance. Making decisions about shoes, makeup, jewelry, and hair, women strove to express their personality, preferences, and style.

Such self-expression included efforts to present themselves as female preachers. Since gender is an aspect of selfhood, choices about shoes, makeup, jewelry, and hair happened in conjunction with their manifestations of womanhood. Here history and contemporary culture played a role. In every historical era female preachers have presented themselves, in some fashion, like women. In previous centuries female preachers' clothed and adorned appearance had either cast them as virtuous women, minimized their femininity in favor of a more masculine persona, or attempted to transcend the dilemmas of embodiment altogether. If a female preacher did dress explicitly as a sexually available woman, she risked creating controversy around her alluring look. Today's female preacher inhabits a more expansive, variable, public space, with greater freedom to draw out the multiple elements socially associated with the feminine. Even with wider space in which to do so, clergywomen in this study debated how best to incorporate femininity into their appearance, most reliably looking toward accessories as the markers of being female. The group added color to their wardrobes, wore jewelry, experimented with shoe styles, and frequented beauty salons. They sought their own ways of being a female preacher, with adornment decisions serving as maneuvers to negotiate how to best present themselves *as themselves* in the pulpit.

A lived body approach argues that the self evolves amid an individual's unique resolution of physicality, particular culture, and individual choice. A person's embodied existence, which contains an ever-shifting core of meanings that comprise a sense of "being me," is constantly being developed and redeveloped through the culturally influenced, physically-structured decisions about how to dress, adorn, present, and move one's body. While their self-understanding as preachers was formed by a myriad of embodied actions, the question of "being me" or "being a female preacher" crystallized within the decisions of adornment. As women added elements to their clothes, they listened to the internal motivations guiding their choices. They characterized a choice for a certain type of shoe or a particular hairstyle as a statement about the self, learning more about their actions as they experienced the choice while preaching and received the congregation's reactions. Because adornment selections were specific to an individual, the ability to bring the embodiments of everyday life into preaching was highly valued. Above all, women sought consistency between their bodily lives out of the pulpit and in it.

Debates around Self-Expression in the Pulpit

Analyzing adornment decisions introduced questions about how self-expression factors into preaching. The claim that "God made me to be a woman and called me to preach as a woman" was a self-identifying claim. Furthermore, a preacher is not just a female while preaching but also her female self in the office during the week, at home in the evening or weekends, and around the neighborhood. Many adornments entering the pulpit were utilized in these other spaces and the ability to successfully join the spheres gave flesh to the claim of "being me." Maintaining continuity in their embodiments across roles and places was vital for these women. It served as an avenue for feeling confident in their preaching identity, as a means by which they linked their selfhood and their preaching.

Homiletical conversations about the preacher's selfhood, or identity, have typically veered in two directions. Scholars have expounded on the organizing motif of a preacher, be it as a herald, storyteller, pastor, or witness.[1] Alternatively, scholars have delved into the character of the preacher,

1. Long, *Witness of Preaching*, 18–51.

exploring the concept of ethos. Ethos developed within ancient rhetoric to signify "the trustworthiness of the speaker," which served as one of many "proofs" to verify a speech.[2] For these preachers, discussions about ethos emerged in a congregation's reception of a preacher's adornments. A more recent homiletical study defined ethos as "the role that the listener's perception of the speaker" played in the overall communication.[3] A preacher's choices for a short haircut, dangling earrings, or brown loafers could affect the congregation's characterization of her as a preacher, which, in turn, can either advance or hinder the sermon's reception.[4] The scholars studying listeners renamed ethos as something akin to presence, which they defined as "a nebulous and hard to grasp quality which tended to cluster around the perception of the connection of the preacher to God, the demeanor of the preacher . . . and the perception that the preacher has confidence and authority."[5] While these women didn't employ the same language when discussing either their decisions or their congregations' responses, they did sense the dual and at times competing tasks of accurately representing themselves as themselves and fulfilling the listeners' expectations about their character or authority to preach.

The same scholars who defined ethos as presence elaborate on the role of identification within preaching. Identification signifies the connections between preacher and listener, specifically born in those moments when the ones in the pews recognized something in the speaker.[6] The preacher's efforts to forge a relationship with the congregation, by evidencing familiarity, accessibility, or similarity to those listening, strengthen the message's reception if the identification was successful.[7] Congregations demonstrated such identification processes at work as they complimented and criticized the preacher's adornments, making these decisions a possible avenue for identification. Because many adornments could be classified as feminine markers—culturally approved (or not) ways of being a woman—the dilemmas around this set of decisions illuminated the female preachers' attempts

2. Edwards, *History of Preaching*, 12.

3. McClure et al., *Listening to Listeners*, 8.

4. Ibid.

5. Mulligan, *Believing in Preaching*, 56.

6. McClure et al., *Listening to Listeners*, 15.

7. McClure et al. assert, "Listeners respond better and listen more closely to a preacher with whom they have a real or perceived connection" (ibid., 15).

to create an effective presence and a sturdy line of identification with their listeners.

Three Adornments: Shoes, Hairstyles, and Fingernail Polish

Although jewelry and makeup represented common identifying markers, both of these adornments received scant attention and a minimalist approach. Most preachers wore varying degrees of makeup and when asked about preaching preparations, did not delve into the topic. Choosing jewelry raised practical considerations about necklaces poking out under albs or dangling earrings interfering with microphones. Instead, preachers gravitated to shoes, hairstyles, and fingernail polish as complicated, thought-provoking areas for discernment. Shoes were the element of clothing most noticed under robes and often named as a place for self-expression. Hair was an extension of the body, signaling everything from personal preference to ethnicity, from professional demeanor to age. Female preachers spoke about their hairstyling decisions at length, frequently seeing their hair as a symbol of their negotiations with their congregations. To paint one's fingernails, and in what color, emerged as a surprisingly complex decision. Preachers weighed the appropriate colors for the pulpit alongside a desire for trendy nails. Believing that self-expression happened through adornment, this chapter will look closely at these three areas.

The choices around shoes, hair, and fingernail polish illuminated the bundles of internal and external norms related to but distinct from general clothing norms. While the clothing decisions discussed thus far were linked to established standards, choices of adornment waded into murkier waters filled with ad hoc rules, anecdotal standards, and contradictory advice. The choices connected to accessories were experienced as personalized choices, even as culture and context played a role in a woman's discernment about what kind of preacher she presented and what kind of preacher she hoped to embody. All of those decisions stayed in tension with an abiding belief, as Rev. Anderson so aptly stated, that "God called me to be who I am, as a preacher and a female preacher."

Beyond the Shoe Boundaries

When preaching day came, many women drew from a small array of shoe options. Rev. Baker reported, "I wear traditional pumps, patent leather in the summer and black in the winter." Ms. Clark said, "I wear one of my three sets of flats: a black pair, a navy pair, and a brown pair." Rev. Lewis added. "I wear very conservative colors, lots of black and navy blue. I wear flats because I am not good in heels. To me, it is just part of the uniform." Many women in this study agreed with their choices, describing the shoes in their closets as "regulation pumps" or "Sunday shoes." They relied upon these plain, dark- or neutral-colored, low-heeled or flat shoes to anchor their preaching attire. Rev. Baker explained, "I'm very conscious of the shoes I wear because they are the one thing that shows. And I find that people do comment on my shoes." These shoes were an extension of professional attire, held to the same standards of good grooming and unobtrusive form. Like clerical robes and skirt suits, they conveyed credibility, dependability, and authority, even as they minimized the opportunity for personalized style.[8]

Amid the instances of wearing the standard "preacher's shoes" were occasions when women chose distinctive elements or non-uniform shoes. Rev. Baker donned traditional pumps, but she favored riskier heels. "I do wear thin, stiletto, two-inch heels, because that is what I like," she said. Rev. Harris once chose red, open-toed heels for Pentecost Sunday and painted her toenails red to match. Preaching in the summer months, Rev. Martin slipped on white sandals with gold accents while Rev. Anderson selected black sandals with tiny white ribbons. Each choice represented the preacher's tastes and personality, a small acknowledgment of the unique self amid her overall embodiment.

Rev. Williams's self-expression manifested through removing her shoes for preaching. "I preach barefoot because I really think that preaching is a very holy place to be. It is the time I am the most excited and the most terrified," she said. "I'm a very tactile person and so that physical reminder is very helpful to me. It literally and figuratively grounds me." Entering and exiting the pulpit in a pair of exemplary preaching shoes, she slips them off during the prayer before the sermon. Her congregation noticed when she lost two inches between prayer and preaching. She explained her behavior. "Some people said 'that's really cool,'" she continued. "Some joked that they were going to take up a collection to buy me shoes that fit. But it has been well-received." While another congregation might have interpreted the removal of shoes differently, associating bare feet with informality or

8 Fischer-Mirkin states, "Mid-heeled conservative pumps indicate reliability, dignity, and refinement" (*Dress Code*, 212).

inappropriate allure, her church affirmed her method of entering into sacred space. In this situation, her listeners' respect for her choice aided Rev. Williams's sense of "being me" while preaching.

While women could encounter listeners who affirmed—or did not comment—on their personalized choices, there existed other moments when the preacher's shoes generated feedback. Although it was rare for congregants to criticize shoe choices, several women found, like Rev. Baker, that listeners commented upon their shoes. Such comments reinforced a familiar experience within women's narratives around the ever-present objective gaze focused on their appearance.[9] Furthermore, if a personalized choice—a moment of "being me"—was critiqued, then the criticism risked landing as a comment about one's preaching self. One woman was forced to respond in a moment when "being me" received a less than hospitable reception.

One morning, Rev. Walker selected red ballet flats to match her red jacket as she prepared for worship. Her red shoes were visible beneath her robe as she stood at the table to celebrate Holy Communion. The older women who occupied the sanctuary's back pew did not come forward to receive the bread and cup. The next morning, they lodged a complaint about her shoes with the senior pastor. They could not participate in communion they said, because her red shoes had profaned the sacred meal.

Rev. Walker was embarrassed by the complaints and the awkward conversation between herself and the senior pastor that followed. She linked the rejection of her shoes to assumptions about her body. Asked what she thought motivated the complaints, she replied, "There is still living among us a generation of women who identify certain objects as scandalous: red shoes, stilettos, or pointed-toed shoes. These symbols of harlotry have great power for those older women." Her shoes communicated to the back pew about her sexuality or character. "At the time I thought it was just plain silly and bad theology to boot," she continued. But years later, she named the symbolic associations at work in society and church. "We do transmit our cultural baggage into theological understanding," she suggested. "In my closet I have three pairs of red flat shoes and two pairs of heeled red boots. I wear them with pride, but I would never wear them in worship." Although extreme, Rev. Walker's red shoes illustrated the risks of embodiments

---

9. The sense of having her body closely observed and evaluated is well documented. See Young, *On Female Body Experience*; Lawless, *Holy Women*; Sentilles, *Church of Her Own*.

labeled dangerously feminine, provocatively sexual, or potentially scandalous. Rev. Walker had chosen shoes that coordinated with her outfit. While
not believing any shoes had the power to defile the sacrament, she then
adjusted the boundary around shoes for preaching.

As an aspect of how women dressed their bodies, shoes held symbolic
power for preachers and parishioners. They did theological work, most
readily discernible through bare feet that evoked Moses's removal of his
sandals before the burning bush. Each style, whether red shoes, plain black
pumps, or jeweled summer sandals, enfleshed a diversity of preaching
bodies and communicated that this particular body, in its specificity and
preferences, could bring God's word. Although certain shoes received more
attention, all of these shoes could be characterized as feminine shoes. The
listeners' reaction to the preacher's shoes contributed to a women's development of her preaching identity. A compliment about the shoes felt like a
welcome of their femaleness. A criticism made a woman wonder whether
or not the critique extended beyond her shoes to her self. Whatever the
message, a congregation's response enabled a preacher to learn more how
she embodied her preaching.

Many of the shoes women considered wearing while preaching were
ones they wore with ease in other situations. Bringing those shoes into sacred space functioned to bring other aspects of the self into the preaching
role. Rev. Walker spoke admiringly of a colleague who deliberately wore
"high, high heels" for her ordination service. This minister, acting against
the advice of others, selected her favorite style of shoes, which could be
viewed as extremely feminine or slightly scandalous, in this pivotal moment
to signify that she was being who she truly was on that occasion. Explaining
her choice several months later, the preacher said, "I deliberately chose the
shoes because I wanted to be me on such an important occasion. But I also
wanted the church, by ordaining me in those shoes, to bless all of me." She
wanted to be embraced as herself, equipped and authorized for ministry in
all the glory of her embodied life. The ways in which listeners and preachers
negotiated such an embracement of embodiment came more clearly into
view as women turned to the next set of adornment deliberations, deciding
how to style their hair.

Hair: Negotiating a Preacher's Identity

Rev. Robinson had always struggled with her hair. Although she aimed to dress in a way that took her appearance off the table, she found her hair worked against her goal. "As far as hair [goes], I feel like I'm entering into a skill set I don't have. I just wish someone would come in and fix my hair," she said, laughing. "I'm not ever really happy with it." Her honey-brown hair was cut in a short pixie cut, with loose layers that made it easier to air-dry but also vulnerable to hanging in various directions. She often ran her fingers through her hair as she preached, and "unless it is shellacked into place," it became disheveled during the sermon. "There have been times when I have literally thought what have I done to my hair?" she said. "What does it look like right now?"

One Sunday following worship, a congregant approached her to say, "Your hair is really distracting." Embarrassed by his comment, Rev. Robinson replied with a good-humored, "my hair is my hair," while privately questioning the appropriateness of the comment. She wondered if a "congregation would ever find a man's hair distracting." Her experience illustrated the close scrutiny of female bodies and the impact of such critical observations on any preacher. Acknowledging that women in public roles are held to a higher standard of appearance than their male counterparts, Rev. Robinson longed for "the equivalent of a hair robe I could put on in the morning and just have it done."

Rev. Robinson's desire for a stronger skill set and her encounter with a complaint about distraction introduce the dilemmas involved with hair. Hair, as an extension of the body, was an inescapable aspect of preaching preparations. Women worked diligently to settle upon hairstyles that felt representative of themselves, their preaching role, and their congregation's expectations. "I worry about my hair more than anything else about my appearance," said Rev. Harris, citing her dark, curly hair. Unlike shoes, the choices in hairstyles were not governed by a prevailing standard or "hair robe" equivalent. No two preachers wore identical hairstyles. Their individual decisions were shaped by age, life stage, hair type and texture, personal preference, congregational context, and larger cultural influences. Hair served as a conversation topic between preacher and listener, as listeners commented upon certain hairstyles and preachers pondered how to interpret their remarks. Over time, women's self-expression through hair became an avenue through which women negotiated their preaching selves.

John S. McClure employs the phrase "negotiating a hearing" to name the ongoing inter-communication between preacher and listener in which the preacher specifically utilizes language, symbols, images, interpretative methods, and cultural cues to make receptive space for the sermon.[10] The preacher's embodiment participates in the negotiation. Within this study, exchanges around hair demonstrated how a preacher's particular habitations helped shape the preacher-listener relationship. Every preacher developed her own habitations around her hair. Shoes possessed an equivalent shoe robe into which preachers could retreat as necessary. In contrast, one could not turn one's unique hair into anything resembling a blank slate. As women searched for the right hairstyle for themselves and their preaching contexts, the process illuminated the desire for self-expression as it met the negotiation at work between pulpit and pew.

Hair is one of the human body's most versatile raw materials.[11] Standing between nature and culture, hair comes with a particular color, texture, thickness, and curl (or lack thereof). We then manipulate these raw materials through coloring, shaping, curling, straightening, or decorating.[12] Historically, hair also has served as a distinguishing marker between male and female bodies. Women's hair has almost always been worn longer than men's. It has been linked to evaluations of feminine beauty, symbolizing anything from attractiveness to sexual seduction.[13] In centuries past, married Christian and Jewish woman were expected to keep their hair long, but wear it bound and covered.[14] During recent centuries, what has been deemed fashionable for hair has varied from elaborate hairstyles reserved for women of leisure during the Renaissance to the short "bob" of the 1920s liberated woman, from the layered shag of the 1970s to the power haircuts of the 1980s.[15] With no single hairstyle currently dominating the landscape, these contemporary preachers chose from a range of options. Experiencing hair as elemental to their bodily life, they made choices that evoked the self.[16]

10. McClure, *Four Codes of Preaching*, 12.

11. Stevenson, "Hairy Business," 137.

12. Ibid.

13. Weitz, *Rapunzel's Daughters*, xv. See Fisher-Mirkin, *Dress Code*, 225; Stevenson, "Hairy Business," 139–40.

14. Weitz, *Rapunzel's Daughters*, 4.

15. Ibid., 5–19, 120.

16. Weitz writes, "Growing directly out of our bodies, our hair often seems magically emblematic of our selves" (ibid., xiv).

For Rabbi Kahn, hair served as an avenue for self-assertion as well as a starting point for conversation. Serving in the same small congregation over several years, she presented a variety of hair lengths and colors during her ministry. In the early years, her wavy, brown hair fell around her shoulders. One year she grew her hair until it hung midway down her back, intending to donate hair to the nonprofit *Wigs for Kids*. She knew some "people would prefer me to have shorter hair." Over the months, congregational members commented, "Rabbi, your hair is getting really long." She hoped the criticism inherent in the comment would be altered by her reply. "I'm growing it to cut it off for a wig," she said. "I need ten inches to cut and ten inches to keep." More recently, Rabbi Kahn shifted her hair color from brown to red. She enjoyed altering her hue, finding it a fun outlet to "be herself." Again, the new hair prompted responses within her congregation. "Anytime I change the color, people notice," she said. "Seventh grade girls will say, 'Oh, Rabbi, you've changed your hair. We love it!'" She continued, "I think people who comment on hair, it is their way of connecting to us. I feel people don't know how to approach us or connect to us, so they pick something that is obvious like hair and comment on it, because that is what they would do in their social settings with their girl friends." Rabbi Kahn's hair choices, which she altered based on her interests and inclinations, ushered additional aspects of her self into her preaching role. Her congregation engaged in dialogue with her about this facet of her embodiment. In this instance, no conflict emerged between the preacher's choices and the congregation's expectations. Instead continuity between pulpit life and larger life deepened a connection between preacher and listener. A seemingly surface conversation about hair might serve as a testing ground for the woman occupying the rabbi's role, as both preacher and listener played with what a preacher might look like and, by extension, who a preacher might be.

In a similar process, Rev. Martin's varying hairstyles narrated the development of her preaching place within a new church. When she arrived as the first female pastor, Rev. Martin fielded questions about her age, experience, and skills. In her thirties with younger children, she characterized her presentation as "elegant, simple, and stylish." During her first weeks of preaching, she noticed different reactions to assorted hairstyles. "When it is up in a ponytail, people think I am young," she said. When Rev. Martin pulled back her hair into a bun, the questions about age decreased but did not disappear entirely. So she started parting her hair in the middle and having it fall straight to her shoulders. This style garnered the fewest comments, the least amount of critiques, and, over time, emerged as the style most likely to be well received by her congregation. She settled on this style, which met her self-expressive needs and calmed her congregation's anxiety. Rev. Martin's experimentation with several hairstyles mimicked a hesitant congregation trying out the new minister. Doubts about her character or competence formed into questions about her gender and youthfulness. Questions about her youthfulness or gender, in turn, were transformed into criticism about youthful hair. This ongoing dialogue was congregationally specific, as the final hairdo Rev. Martin adopted—freely flowing to the shoulders—had prompted comments about age, gender, or single status when worn by Rabbi Kahn.

In addition to being altered by the particularities of a congregation, the habits of hair have varied widely by ethnic and racial groups. Second only to skin, hair serves as a racial signifier.[17] Within the African American community, hairstyles, and the meanings invested in them, emerge from the history of slavery in America, as well as the practices within African and free African American cultures. Often measured against the white ideal of long, straight, blond hair, African American females made decisions about styling their hair keenly aware that their choices could be interpreted as an assertion of the self or as an indication of white American culture's suppressive influence.[18] Calling her hair "more than the proverbial crowning glory," Rev. Walker affirmed hair as an available means through which to express pride as well as to exercise agential power.[19] She understood her hair choices as rooted in identity politics yet also based on personal preferences about the style that best suited her.[20] She and another African American preacher described their decisions to "go natural" with their hair. Going natural served as a means by which they embodied a "this is me" message and drew their congregations into the conversation.

Rev. Lewis kept her tightly curled hair cut close to the head. She framed the style as one that evolved gradually through years of gaining appreciation for being herself. "I used to wear my hair long," she said. "Then I wore a bob. I wore short but straight hair for a little while." This style, she

17. Banks, *Hair Matters*, 8.

18. Weitz, *Rapunzel's Daughters*, 9.

19. Weitz notes that hair was "one of the few means available to black slaves for expressing pride and identity" (ibid., 9).

20. Banks concludes from her research that the hairstyle choices of African American women are "a medium to understand complex identity politics that intersect along the lines of race, gender, class, sexuality, power, and beauty" (148).

noted, pointing to her head, was the product of the wisdom that comes with age. Finally, she said, "I just went natural." The style framed her face, matched her smaller stature, and suited her stage in life. More importantly, her hair communicated her confidence with her embodied self. "I'm pretty much me," she repeated. Going natural was one small but significant way she expressed herself in the pulpit.

Rev. Walker had reached a similar place of ease with her hair, although with a very different hairstyle. "Styling my hair is not a priority for me," she said. "I am gifted with long, thick wonderful hair and I do nothing with it, to the disappointment of others. Many years ago I made a decision to stop putting chemical 'perms' or 'relaxers' in my hair." Often pulling her hair away from the face with a bun, Rev Walker opted for a natural look, citing the "reams written about the significance of hair among American black women" as part of her decision. Her surrounding community did not always agree with her style. "Through the years I have had several [people] offer to pay for me to get my hair fixed," she reported. She consistently re-sisted such suggestions, using the comments to begin conversations about the nexus of meanings existing around hair. All the while, she maintained her hair in its unaltered beauty, presenting a hairstyle that conveyed her comfort in her body, her identity as an African American woman, and her role as a pastor-preacher. Her decisions, as well as the resultant conversa-tions, helped reshape her congregation's expectations for their preacher's hair. It enabled her, like Rev. Lewis, to stand firm in embodying the truth "this is who I am." The phrase "going natural" seemed apt in both narra-tives, a signifier of women maintaining their selfhood while they preached.

The different conversations—and distinct interpretations—attached to each preacher's hair demonstrated how congregational setting, along with the preacher's body type, age, and race, impacted the embodiments of any one woman. Every preacher adopted her own hairstyle. Every congre-gation had their own reactions to the preacher's hair. The ensuing negotia-tions created a meeting place of expectations, critiques, reinterpretations, and hopes. Conversations about hair were rarely just about hair. They were about authority, character, and confidence. They could also be about race, money, and class. The "right" hairstyle could connect preacher and listener, just as the "wrong" one could spark disconnection between pulpit and pew. Since this study explored the preacher's viewpoint, the role of hair in a woman's evolving preaching self—a process distinct from yet always formed in conjunction with her listening congregation—was most easily identifiable.

Rabbi Levin had worn her blond hair in a bob for many years. It was a simple, tidy arrangement she considered appropriate for her facial features and shorter height. Like Rev. Martin, she occasionally pulled it back in a ponytail, hearing comments about looking "a little casual today" from others in the service. During her first years at her congregation, she fielded comments about her need for a haircut. "It didn't matter if I had just gotten a haircut," Rabbi Levin reflected. "I might hear I needed a haircut." Over time, her reaction to the advice changed. "Finally I realized it might not work for everyone, but I wasn't going to go out and . . . get a nice little hair makeover," she said. "I liked my hair just fine."

Arriving at the conclusion "I like my hair" was an important moment of joining one's bodily choices and one's preaching. Lacking a reigning standard and posed at the intersection of nature and culture, hair was uniquely personal. Some aspects of one's hair can be altered. Other elements cannot. As they considered what style worked best for their preaching, women retained their agency. Amid the facts of their hair and the realities of their congregation, they asserted the freedom to decide upon their bodily presentation. Embracing their preferences about their hair enabled women to maintain a sense of self while preaching. This was a claiming of one's bodily life that strengthened the preacher's presence and her capacity to be heard by her listeners.

Fingernails: Expressing Female Beauty

A group of ministerial colleagues gathered for lunch. Sitting down at the table, Rabbi Kahn had fingernails painted in a popular, deep purple color. "That is an awfully dark color," commented another clergywoman. "You wouldn't wear the color to preach, would you?" "Why not?" replied Rabbi Kahn. "Plenty of the moms in my congregation wear it. Why wouldn't I have the same nail color as them?" A short but intense debate ensues over the meal. Most of these women painted their fingernails and toenails. They agreed that fingernail nail color differed from toenail color. A preacher can wear bright or unusual shades on their toes without drawing attention. Fingernails were far more visible. Can one wear dark purple, dusty blue, or black on her hands while preaching? The group became divided between those who regularly wore these colors in the pulpit, those who selected traditional reds or pinks, and those who stuck to neutral nails. All agreed hands were an important part of preaching, a potential asset or distraction. As another clergywoman commented, "What are the limits of color? I don't want people to be distracted, but beautiful hands seem so important."[21]

A preacher's hands, and by extension her fingernails, were an integral part of her preaching. Tidy nails evidenced attention to the body. Rev. Walker reported on her monthly pedicure. "For me, it is self-care," she said. "Not only do I get my feet pampered but that massage chair! And in warm weather, well-tended feet are a must for women." Congregations noticed when nails were not well maintained. "I had a parishioner once tell me how worried she was about my stress level," said Rev. Harris. "And then she pointed to my ripped cuticles." Clean, trimmed nails were a baseline necessity, communicating a present, prepared clergyperson in ways akin to professional attire. They were the foundation of beautiful preaching hands.

When the topic turned to the color of fingernails, opinions differed widely about what made for preaching hands. Rev. Martin limited her polish to earthy tones, wanting to "remain as neutral as possible." Rev. Baker reported, "I wear very traditional colors; pinks and reds. I simply don't like blues, greens, and blacks. I am a traditional kind of gal." Rev. Walker favored red tones like cinnamon, outliers on the classic spectrum. "Black people expect women, including pastors, to have lovely hair and nails. It's in the culture," she elaborated. One preacher embraced the purple, blue, and black tones that prompted the lunchtime debate. "I preach with black nails," said Rabbi Kahn. While others questioned her choice, she maintained her nail color, reiterating, "This color is fine." Her refusal to alter her nails was a moment of self-expression, a resistance to a colleague's or congregant's attempt to control her embodied choices.

Whether they wore neutral, classic, or modern colors, women expressed affinity for their choice. Personal preference guided their decisions. Women explained their color selections as ones that resonated with their sense of who they were, both as women and as preachers. While wearing the expected clerical robes or professional attire, they used their nails to interject their personality, building a bridge between their habits beyond the pulpit and their habits within it. Just as being a preacher was an integral element of who they were, being someone "just like other moms" or someone who kept current with fashion trends was vital to their selfhood. Nail

---

21. Weinstein, "Your Preachin' and Pastorin' Paws."

color was a small, telling space to insert individuality—the power of their embodied self—into proclamation.

Nail polish is a feminine marker. Some nail colors are judged, by some, to be provocative, inappropriate, or inappropriately alluring for preaching. But while the habitations around the sexually transgressing preacher might lend interpretive insight, a stronger lens by which to characterize this conversation is as one about beauty. By implying that beautiful hands are important, the women were deliberating about the aesthetic potential of a preaching body. They wanted the freedom to have beautiful hands. The end they sought was not glamour but the capacity for their particular, living, embodied selves to be the vehicle for holy proclamation, akin to Paul's words in Romans, "How beautiful are the feet [or the hands] of those who bring good news."[22]

Can I Be Me: Continuity In and Out of the Pulpit

The female preachers' decisions around adornment were decisions about how to embody their evolving selves. Through the process of choosing a hairstyle, shoes, or fingernail color, a woman pondered how to express herself in the pulpit, fulfilling the desire to "look like the woman God created her to be." Her adornments spurred conversations between preacher and listeners, providing an avenue by which the space for her preaching body was negotiated and often expanded. Adornment decisions, by conveying something of who the preacher is, illustrated the ways in which the depth of embodied life is brought into the sermon.

Woven through these stories is a common thread of women seeking congruence between adornments worn with ease outside the pulpit and adornments acceptable for preaching. Women wanted to wear the shoes they liked, adopt the hairstyle that felt natural to them, and keep the fingernail polish they selected on Monday on their nails for the weekend. The power within these decisions came from an adornment's capacity to represent the continuity of self in and beyond preaching. Rabbi Levin articulated her sense of this need when answering the question "What is your best vision for yourself in the pulpit?" She said,

> I think by being a real person that people can relate to, whether it
> is a wife or mother or as a woman. I've become much more aware

22. Rom 10:15b NRSV.

of being a real person and how people relate to that by trying to be consistent both on and off the bema. That is something that is really important to me—that what I speak about is how I live. It is really important to me to be consistent with the messages I give both on and off the bema. And how I present myself.

Choices of shoes, hairstyles, and fingernail polish assisted in the building of consistency on and off the bema. They gave material expression to a preacher's capacity to "be a real person" while preaching.

The name homiletical scholarship gives to a preacher's effective capacity to merge the multiple worlds she inhabits into a "real" preaching presence is sincerity. Sincerity defines the correspondence between a woman's thoughts, preferences, and personality and how she represents herself as a preacher.[23] A sincere preacher is a truthful preacher, who is "consistent in how she speaks and how she lives."[24] The greater the consistency, the more sincere the preacher.

While sincerity can and has been orchestrated, listeners watch a preacher for evidence of her sincerity.[25] Historically, sincerity has been judged through an analysis of delivery, a topic to be covered in the next chapter. For the women of this study, issues around sincerity also linked to adornments. The sincere preacher held constant her adornments across the multiple spheres she inhabited. Her choices for dress and adornments, though, were influenced by culture and especially by the social construction of gender. Simply put, it was challenging, at times, for female preachers to create totally consistent self-presentations in and out of the pulpit. Encountering different norms for the various social roles they inhabited, they experienced those norms varying widely from sphere to sphere. They navigated how to express femininity, which could mean one set of adornments on Friday evening and an alternate set on Sunday morning. And they contended with the specific expectations existing within a congregation about a preacher's presentation. Red shoes, free-flowing hairstyles, and colorful nails could be a source of embodied strength. They could also precipitate conflict if a listener's critique of her embodiment prompted a woman to lessen the continuity within her embodied self. When the adornments by which the preacher embodied sincerity felt strained, then she might wonder how she could embody sincerity at all.

23. Smith, *New Measures*, 189–91.

24. Ibid., 188–89.

25. For a description of orchestrating sincerity, see Smith, *New Measures*, 182–220.

Merleau-Ponty argues, "We are in the world through our body . . . by thus remaking contact with the body and with the world we shall also rediscover ourself."[26] These preachers believed God created them to be themselves in the world, preachers and women and women preachers. Adornment deliberations taught them more about the spheres they inhabited, the cultures in which they negotiated preaching embodiments, and who they wanted to be as preachers. While still discovering themselves, they moved from adornment decisions to considerations of their voice and movement while preaching. Here they encountered a similar set of dilemmas around authority, sincerity, and natural congruence.

26. Merleau-Ponty, *Phenomenology of Perception,* 236.

CHAPTER 5

The Natural Performance
and the Female Preacher

On a bright spring Sunday morning, Ms. Melissa Clark preached her final sermon in the congregation where she had served as a ministerial intern. The multiuse sanctuary resembled an auditorium. Her pulpit was a portable music stand. She delivered her sermon, titled "God Is Leading Us," with a clear, strong voice registering in the middle ranges. Ms. Clark preached from behind the music stand, moving in front of it whenever she shifted into an illustration. Her body mimed walking alongside her grandmother into church. Her arms mimicked a boat rocking on the water. Ms. Clark occasionally thought about her gestures prior to preaching, but when asked, she could not recall a specific instance of planning her actions. "I don't feel embodied when I preach," she reflected. "I don't even feel like I have legs." Her body, of course, was an integral aspect of her sermon. Her hands were especially noticeable. They moved excitedly when she emphasized a sermonic point. They gestured outward toward the congregation during a key transition. With posture, position, voice, and hands she brought her sermon to life, conveying her message through her physical form.

Historically a preacher's use of voice and gestures has been considered under the category of delivery. Originating in ancient rhetoric, delivery designated "an art of gestures and vocal modulations that the orator typically composed along with the content of the speech."[1] Delivery played a crucial role in a sermon's overall effectiveness as an essential means by which a

1. Mountford, *Gendered Pulpit*, 5–6.

sermon is proclaimed. In more recent years, scholars have broadened the subject to consider a preacher's performance.[2] Often borrowing insights from theater, performance encompasses "both the verbal shape and the physical embodiment" a preacher brings to proclamation.[3] A sermon truly becomes a sermon when a preacher's embodiment brings it to life.

Ms. Clark's vocal and gestural behaviors, as well as her reflections about them, introduced the contradictory landscape experienced by these women when the topic turned to performance. On one hand, they recognized the significance of their voice and movements. Rev. Harris said, "Preaching is an act of drama. How I use my body, my hands and my voice, that matters." Rabbi Levin said, "People expect a sermon to be elevated. There is a different element. I think about my voice. I want to add, not forced gestures, but gestures." Rev. Baker added, "I think of my body as a vehicle. It is employing everything I have to get the message across." At the same time, women also articulated the challenges of utilizing their bodies to achieve a sermon's fullest expression. Rev. Robinson reflected, "I'm trying to be more comfortable with gestures and moving. Early in my nervous days, I was much more wooden vocally and physically." Rev. Robinson's hesitancy was of a practical order. For others, the challenge was conceptual in nature. Rabbi Levin added to her reflections, "To a certain degree, I feel like when I'm up there [on the bema] I have to act. And I'm not necessarily comfortable with acting. I mean acting beyond who I am." The task of bringing a sermon to life through speech and action proved an inspiring yet daunting task complicated by questions about bodies, movements, and the best performances.

The Rise of Performance in Homiletics

In the last quarter of the twentieth century, homiletics took a turn toward performance.[4] Prior to this turn, voice, posture, and movement were organized under the category of delivery, which concerned "the preacher's act

2. Most scholars mark the shift from predominately delivery language to more performance-centered language to the 1980's shifts toward narrative preaching. However, delivery is still used often as a way to talk about a preacher's use of her voice and body. Delivery and performance occupy overlapping arenas, as performance can encompass delivery but can also include any aspect of the preacher's bodily life in relationship to a sermon.

3. Shuster, "Truth and Truthfulness," 24.

4. See Childers, *Performing the Word*, 42–43; Allen, *Preaching*, 107.

of bringing thought to expression."[5] Utilizing the structure of ancient rhetoric, delivery was deemed one of five necessary stages in speech. Preaching manuals addressed the body's impact on the sermon, often exploring how posture, gestures, and voice work as tools that enhance communication.[6] Performance, in contrast, asserted the integral and inseparable role embodiment plays in every sermon, from the initial forays into scripture all the way through the final proclamation. Although the concept of delivery is still utilized in homiletical conversations, performance adds insights into how a sermon "achieves completion when it is 'enfleshed' by means of the voice and body of the speaker."[7]

Performance in preaching arises from the belief that embodied life is a continuous enactment, a dramatic stream of behaviors that are meaning filled and meaning making.[8] As bodily acts, sermons are performances. Here a preacher gives "his or her body and voice to the text for the purpose of bringing it to life in a particular context."[9] The preacher's enfleshment is grounded, within Christian theology, in God's speech-act of the incarnation, which is a performative event.[10] A preacher, whose body serves as a site of God's presence, brings form and word together for the purposes of proclamation.[11] Performance pushes preachers to think beyond the written formulation of a sermon to the critical moment when it is communicated to a congregation. Sermons require embodiment, asserts Charles L. Bartow, for "to be fully known, they must be performed."[12]

The preachers of this study articulated how they performed sermons, even as they hesitated to use the word performance. Women identified their bodies as a tool, vehicle, or vessel for gaining sacred knowledge. "If we are created in the image of God," said Rabbi Levin, "then our bodies are

5. Bartow, "Delivery of Sermons," 100–101.

6. For an overview of gestures in preaching, see Edwards, *History of Preaching*, 210–38, 391–463. For an application of the historic teachings about the body in preaching, see Walters, "Body in the Pulpit," 445–62.

7. Bozarth-Campbell, *Word's Body*.

8. Ward, "Performance Turns in Homiletics." See Schechner, *Performance Theory*; Turner, *Ritual Process*. Schechner asserts that every aspect of life is meaningful drama, while Turner's studies of ritual illuminate how the very acts that comprise human existence are performances.

9. Childers, *Performing the Word*, 49.

10. McKenzie, "At the Intersection," 55.

11. Bartow, *God's Human Speech*, 111.

12. Bartow, "Delivery of Sermons," 99.

part of how we get closer to God. The way we use that body brings us closer to God. I definitely see the body as a vessel, God's instrument to do God's will in the world." Building upon similar ideas, Rev. Harris expressed, "In preaching you are an embodied word. And so there is a performance aspect to it. It is not a performance, but you are exposed, you are vulnerable and you are doing something profound. In our tradition, you are proclaiming the Word of God." For both women, the body could be understood, to use Bartow's phrase, as "God's human speech."

At the same time, applying the language of performance to preaching can cause suspicion. Rev. Harris articulated several implications of enacting her sermon, while simultaneously stating, "It is not a performance." A performance brings with it connotations of deception, theatrical imagery aimed at an artificial representation. Marguerite Shuster notes the "powerful and negative visceral reaction against construing proclamation of God's Word as a sort of 'performance.'"[13] Scholars who affirm performance in preaching respond to such criticism by suggesting the techniques of theater train a preacher to communicate through her body, employing purposeful movements at the service of the message.[14] Jana Childers argues a performed sermon is an honest offering of the self, providing a "degree of authenticity or sincerity that belies our stereotypic ideas about acting."[15] Rabbi Levin's reflections represented this artifice versus authentic dilemma, as she acknowledged, "you have to act" while preaching, yet she avoided "acting beyond who I am."

The debate between "acting" and "acting beyond who I am" is not new to preaching. It points to a larger conversation concerning how one might utilize strategies for communication while continuing to signal that her voice and actions are her own. The preacher seeking aids to strengthen her performance might consult a preaching manual, finding in its pages the encouragement to "be natural" in the pulpit. In his work *God's Human Speech: A Practical Theology for Proclamation*, Charles Bartow suggests, "All that we do, from toe tip to hairline, ought to appear natural."[16] The advice to be natural, though, introduced its own questions about what moves,

---

13. Shuster, "Truth and Truthfulness," 19.

14. Childers, *Performing the Word*, 47–49.

15. Childers calls this an "honest performance," writing, "A performance, whether it is onstage or in the pulpit, is honest or truthful when the interpreter is making careful use of experience" (ibid., 51).

16. Bartow, *God's Human Speech*, 94.

voices, and postures are natural and for whom. To explore these questions an analysis of the natural preacher is necessary.

The Natural Preacher

Both earlier discussions about delivery and more recent instructions around performance contain the ideal of a natural preacher. In his *History of Preaching*, O. C. Edwards Jr. notes the varying descriptions placed upon early Christian preachers. Citing scholarship from the Spanish Golden Age, he highlights how this era depicted preachers during the apostolic era evidencing "sincerity and plain-speaking" even though the traits were intermixed with a "kind of eloquence and even elegance."[17] With roots in rhetoric, early preaching practices did include a dimension of learned forms. Those acquired moves blended with a natural style, which was emphasized occasionally as preaching developed alongside the growth of the Christian church. Written during the thirteenth century, Waley's *Ars praedicandi* advised that gestures should be used in moderation and that the sermon be familiar enough for the preacher to "easily find language in which to express the gospel naturally and forcefully."[18] In the eighteenth century, John Wesley advocated for preachers to avoid "anything either awkward or affected in gesture, phrase or pronunciation."[19] The nineteenth-century preacher Charles Haddon Spurgeon, in his *Lectures to My Students*, advised, "Our last rule is one that sums up all the others; be natural in your action."[20] Accompanying his instruction with a series of illustrations depicting staged poses, Spurgeon offered the disclaimer that these positions might appear "a little forced," but concluded the postures are "natural, striking and instructive."[21] Natural, it seemed, served as a key criterion for a preacher's performance.

17. Hilary Dansey Smith writes, "On one hand, the apostolic ideal leads to the conclusion that sincerity and plain-speaking are the only acceptable forms of Christian preaching.... On the other hand, if one looks back to the Fathers one finds quite another kind of eloquence, and even elegance" (*Preaching in the Spanish Golden Age*, 94–95).

18. Edwards, *History of Preaching*, 223.

19. Ibid., 446.

20. Spurgeon, *Lectures to My Students*, 318.

21. Ibid., 320. The templates Spurgeon offered were taken directly from another publication on rhetorical delivery. See Austin, *Chironomia*. See also Dana, *New American Selection of Lessons*; Webster, *American Selection of Lessons*.

Contemporary conversations about performance contain a similar ideal. A natural preacher exhibits a harmony between her thoughts and feelings and the aims of the sermon. Her performance is a seamless composition of voice, message, and movement. Ronald J. Allen argues that "preachers should move their hands, arms, and the rest of their bodies in ways that enhance the content of the sermon and that are consistent with their personality."[22] Todd Farley draws upon John Wesley's preaching directive that the hands and the face should "appear to be the mere, natural result, both of the things you speak, and of the affection that moves you to speak them" to reaffirm "that gestures made while preaching should be so married with the words as to be true and sincere, and so as not to appear contrived or 'affected.'"[23] In so doing, her listeners will comment that "the inside does actually match the outside" and "the preacher was truly herself."[24] In this sense, being natural is not just looking comfortable and expressive while preaching but also possessing a congruence of feelings and sermonic aims. The preacher's convictions match her spoken words. The natural preacher, then, is a sincere one.

Although several threads contributed to the linkage between preaching naturally and being a sincere preacher, the largest influence came from a bundle of preaching practices that arose in the early nineteenth century. Amid the revivals that swept through America in the 1820s, 1830s, and 1840s, a series of new measures emerged marking the expressive, emotive, and natural preacher, best exemplified by the preacher Charles Grandison Finney. Ted A. Smith traces these burgeoning practices, beginning with the rapidly changing landscape of the young American democracy. The first decades of the nineteenth century were characterized by increasing geographical mobility and a resultant social mobility.[25] As people traveled away from their established networks of town and home, they encountered newly delineated spheres separating the public and private realms. The private sphere was the realm of home and church.[26] The public sphere represented the arenas of commerce and politics, and required universal,

22. Allen, *Preaching*, 111. Charles Bartow, in "Delivery of Sermons," reiterates the point, saying, "The body should respond to what is thought and felt so that there may be congruence between the inner form and outer form of the experience being shared" (100).

23. Farley, "Use of the Body," 118–19.

24. Allen, *Preaching*, 108.

25. Smith, *New Measures*, 186–87.

26. Ibid., 188.

impersonal speech.[27] The division of spheres, along with the loss of living in what had been smaller, more closed networks, created anxiety about the "public representations of persons" and an "urgency to questions about the gap between public presentations and private reality."[28] How does one judge a person one has never before encountered? The answer, asserts Smith, came through measuring his sincerity.[29]

Sincerity was defined as the harmony of public and private selves.[30] As Smith articulates, individuals held "deep faith in the primacy, naturalness of the self associated with those spaces and relationships they counted as private."[31] The private world was "the realm of truth and authenticity."[32] The sincere speaker brought into the public domain indicators of the private self. Finney accomplished precisely this through his "practices of public sincerity."[33] Recognizing that to display sincerity "required enabling audiences to compare the public and private personas," he sought ways of "noticeably stepping out from behind a public role . . . and making visible a distinct, private self."[34] He spoke in an extemporaneous, conversational style. He was emotionally expressive, able to preach with tears rolling down his face. He replicated the plain talk of ordinary men, emphasizing his commonality to the masses even as his fame skyrocketed. He perfected practices like eye contact, gestures, and personal recounts of one's life story as convincing ways to connect the preacher's private self to the congregation.[35] Finney "manifested those private qualities in a fully public persona," crafting techniques of sincerity that have been replicated by countless preachers.[36]

27. Ibid., 187.
28. Ibid., 188.
29. Ibid., 188–92.
30. Ibid., 188.
31. Ibid., 189.
32. Ibid., 215.

33. Smith writes the belief that "the man is what he was in private" built "a whole world of oppositions: public selves were representations, but private selves were real, public selves were self-conscious fabrications but private selves were natural beings, the public speech of oratory was suspect, but the private speech of conversation was trustworthy" (ibid., 189).

34. Ibid., 193.
35. Ibid., 212.
36. Ibid., 190.

Finney emphasized the necessity for preaching to be natural, writes Smith, "by which he meant that it should be free from self-consciousness."[37] Imbued with God's Spirit and attuned to the congregation, a preacher's emotive experience paved the way for using the right speech and movements. At the same time, a preacher's feelings, speech, and acts while preaching could reshape a preacher's self. In the end, concludes Smith, "Finney modified his private persona to fit the mold formed by his public one," demonstrating how "the private self . . . became a malleable measure."[38] That the private self can be altered over time casts doubt on the possibility of a purely natural manner of preaching. Natural, as a marker of sincerity, is formed by context, history, and a preacher's repeated behaviors.

Contemporary descriptions of preaching naturally bear the imprint of Finney's legacy. Scholars emphasize the need for the preacher's self to shine through the sermon and for gestures to be born of the passions that move one to preach. Finney's specific practices of conversational style, eye contact, and personal narrative endure as present-day practices. When evaluating sermons, Ronald Allen suggests judging "the degree to which the preacher was truly herself."[39] Yet such a natural evaluation becomes suspect if all performances are acquired ones, learned by multiple enactments in a certain culture with its particular standards of "natural" behavior.

Despite the prominence of naturalness in performance discussions, scholarship remains extremely vague about what is natural and for whom. Finney, Whately, Wesley, and Spurgeon were all men of a height that surpassed the pulpit or stood tall upon the stage. Their voices spanned deeper registers and projected well across a congregation. Their gestures reflected, in some fashion, the patterns of maleness particular to their era. The gendered nature of naturalness becomes clearer as one explores the masculine images embedded in preaching manuals. While Mountford correctly points out how "the arts of preaching inscribe this masculine tradition . . . most often through a smooth surface of universal advice," there are other times when the messages are hard to miss.[40] "Let the physical condition be as vigorous as possible," writes John Broadus, praising a "forceful voice with penetrating power."[41] Spurgeon suggests avoiding "the method of enuncia-

37. Ibid.
38. Ibid., 215, 212.
39. Allen, *Preaching*, 108.
40. Mountford, *Gendered Pulpit*, 2.
41. Broadus, *Treatise*, 482, 485.

tion said to be very ladylike [or] delicate."[42] He encourages the preacher to "speak out boldly and command attention at the outset by your manly tones."[43] Female preaching bodies contend with the legacy of masculine naturalness. They are asked to preach naturally, yet what is considered as natural does not always come naturally to them. Their bodies may appear dwarfed in pulpits built for larger physiques. Their voices may sound different than their male colleagues. Their mannerisms may be dissonant in some distinct yet hard-to-articulate ways. Currently the criteria and means of evaluation do not provide for diverse bodies, recognize the different cultural meanings ascribed to certain bodies, or acknowledge the insights of theorists such as Judith Butler who demonstrate how acts formed by culture and repeated over time come to appear natural even as their origins are not natural.

The natural standard within preaching presents as truth the notion that every preacher can tap into a fully sincere and comfortable preaching embodiment. In reality, the natural standard contains a cultural construction of specific bodies, sounds, and gestures registering as natural. These reigning models are both a product of history and deeply gendered in form. Holding these truths, this chapter now will delve more deeply into the experiences of several women as they contemplated their preaching voices and gestures. Examining their choices illuminates the various ways in which women confronted the natural standard and, at times, created performances that felt natural to them.

The Voice of the Preacher: Physicality and the Evolving Self

Rabbi Levin was the niece of a rabbi. She grew up listening to his powerful preaching voice. "My uncle was a 'preacher's preacher,'" she said. "He would get up and preach these forty-five minute sermons, which never felt long to me. He delivered a message that was not fire and brimstone, but was forceful and dynamic." Experiencing a call to the rabbinate as a young adult, she was acutely aware how physically different she was from her uncle and other rabbinical mentors. She was a petite woman with a soft voice. Even after several years of ministerial experience, she remained self-conscious about the sound of her voice. "I am a good writer," said Rabbi Levin. "I write all my sermons out. I am an editor down to the wire. But the delivery

42. Spurgeon, *Lectures to My Students*, 116.
43. Ibid., 121.

side of things has often been my challenge." Rabbi Levin did not doubt her call to ministry or the content of her message. She consistently received praise for her sermons. Instead, she conceived of her challenges as bodily ones. "I wasn't a loud person," she reflected. "I've never had acting or vocal training. I have had to journey to being comfortable with my voice sounding different than the models that I had."

In their book, *Saved from Silence*, Mary Donovan Turner and Mary Lin Hudson argue that female preachers struggle to "come to voice" in their preaching.[44] Viewing voice as a metaphor for agency, they suggest that larger cultural and religious forces can coalesce to suppress a woman's ability to speak. While unique in its breadth and depth, *Saved from Silence* names what other homiletical teachers have also noticed, a particularly intense and complex struggle in female preachers to gain confidence in their preaching voices.[45] As women ventured into seminaries and pulpits, the issues of finding their power to speak deserved sustained attention. But Rabbi Levin's experience told a slightly different story. Although traversing a similar journey toward preaching confidence, the discomfort she encountered with her voice was not related to issues surrounding her identity, sermonic content, or call. Rather, she struggled to adjust her expectations about what constitutes a "preacher's voice." Her hurdles focused on the physicality of her voice, so different in pitch, tone and volume than the preachers most familiar to her. "Coming to voice" for Rabbi Levin was not about acquiring self-assurance in the content of her speech. It was about gaining confidence in the material characteristics of her voice and a skill set to best utilize the voice she had been given.

The voice is one of the body's most powerful instruments. The sound of the voice is shaped by surrounding voices and cultural expectations linked to gender, class, and ethnicity.[46] We literally "speak with our bodies," as the lips, mouth, and larynx are aided by the torso and back to create sound.[47] An instrument in the body's toolbox, the voice is inseparable from one's composite presentation. Rabbi Levin's voice matched her smaller frame; its material characteristics played a role in her preaching. She noted,

> I was never held back or made to think as a woman that I don't have a voice. For me it was always more of a physical issue. I tend

44. Turner and Hudson, *Saved from Silence.*
45. See McGee, *Wrestling with the Patriarchs,* 9.
46. Karpf, *Human Voice,* 4.
47. Ibid., 23.

> to be a soft-spoken person, so the projection of my voice . . . is a
> harder element for me. I grew up with a male voice in my head and
> I don't have a male voice.

These days she longs for vocal training, wanting ways to strengthen her sound. "People comment on my voice all the time," she reported. "Sometimes they say, 'you were a little too soft, I couldn't hear you.' And they say 'you have a beautiful voice.'"

Preachers have long recognized how critical the voice is to their task. Early preaching manuals described the ideal preaching voice as one that was easily heard, clearly understood, and encompassing a wide range of tones, rates, and volumes.[48] It was a resonant voice, filled with animation. These prescriptions articulate the same need for naturalness. Christine Parton asserts, "The voice is the vehicle for the message. Without a dynamic, natural voice, it is difficult to obtain and maintain the attention of the listener."[49] She adds, "Voice production should be a natural and effortless task."[50] Bartow described the ideal voice as "supple . . . so that what is felt by the preacher may be sounded as clearly as possible," replicating the link between expressing emotions and appearing sincere.[51] These representations of the natural voice rest upon a hidden essentialism, a trust in the voice as part of a person's unchanging core. In reality the voice is part of the living body, formed over time as the preacher's given physical traits interact with its wider culture, the preacher makes choices about how to speak, and draws meanings about one's voice.

The dilemma for Rabbi Levin came with the standard created by other men's voices, a standard by which she judged her own voice and to which her voice would never meet. While her uncle's deeper, more forceful voice counted as the natural preacher's voice, she also preached with a natural voice. Her voice met the criteria of being consistent with her personality and expressive of the affections that led to her sermon. The first women

48. Edwards, *History of Preaching*, 12–14. Also, Edwards draws from his own work on Waleys. He asserts Waleys's advice was that the "preacher should speak neither too loudly or too softly, nor should his voice go up and down in a singsong way. And the preacher should avoid speaking so fast that no one understands what he says. Waleys is opposed to memorizing sermons; rather their substance should be so familiar that the preacher can easily find language in which to express the gospel naturally and forcefully" (223).

49. Parton, "Voice," 495.

50. Ibid.

51. Bartow, "Delivery of Sermons," 100.

who ventured to speak in public were subject to criticism about their voices, which were ridiculed as being too high, too feminine, or too shrill.[52] Contemporary preachers encountered such critiques in more subtle forms, like Rev. Harris's congregants who couldn't hear her during her first weeks. Such comments can be an indication of issues around volume or intelligibility on the part of the preacher or a sign about a congregation's readiness to receive a female preacher. Coming into her preaching voice for Rabbi Levin and others entailed gaining comfort in its physical traits, acquiring the necessary communication skills, and contending with cultural expectations for how a preacher's voice should sound. Female preachers help widen the range of voices that preach, and thus create a diversity of preacherly sounds. Exposing the contextual conditioning behind any voice, they expand the natural standard and, hopefully, preach with their own, natural voice.

Rev. Walker identified her voice as "a strong voice." She credited her childhood church's multiple preachers for insuring she "didn't grow up thinking there was only one right way to preach." She also cherished the growing societal space for vocal diversity. While she did employ "black preaching cadence," she said, "I'm careful about it because I don't want people to think I'm trying to sound like a black male preacher." She continued, "I am so glad that I came along at a time when I knew that I didn't need to sound like Martin Luther King Jr. And I don't. I have my own voice. It is a woman's voice." Not tied to a standard and not wanting to sound like other male preachers, Rev. Walker had developed her voice. For her and other women a natural preaching voice was formed by a combination of physicality, personality, and lived experience. It was a woman's voice, but more importantly it was her voice. Ms. Clark agreed. She said, "I think of my voice as *my* voice. It is akin to the voice I hear in my head. The extent to which my voice is female has to do with truth-telling about my own life as a wife and mother, the sort of things that elicit *amens* from other women in the congregation." These two women guarded against an over-identification with a woman's voice, instead preferring to claim their particular materiality, their voice, as a tool in their preaching.

Discussions around having a "woman's voice" have dominated theoretical discussions for several decades, appearing in communication

---

52. Karpf writes that the first female voices on public broadcasting were reported to irritate many listeners as "they talked too rapidly, over-emphasized unimportant words or tried to impress listeners by talking beautifully" (158).

studies, gender analyses, feminist theory, and preaching. Various homiletical studies have proposed a loose set of characteristics that typify the
female preacher's communication style while other studies blend those
qualities with the process of coming to speech.[53] Each reiteration of how
women speak in distinctive ways enabled greater awareness that the reigning preaching voices were shaded by the maleness of the speakers. But to
promote a voice strongly identified with feminine qualities, whether by its
sound, style, or speech content, provides only a limited alternative. Both
Rabbi Levin's higher, softer, gentler voice and Rev. Walker's louder, firmer,
and deeper one are the voices of female preachers. Each preacher adjusted
to her voice, honing its skills for proclamation. At different times, each acknowledged the femaleness of her voice. It may be that language around
"preaching with a woman's voice" appears in those moments when preachers felt the need to distinguish themselves from male models. And it may
be that the motif of a woman's voice becomes exceptionally salient when life
events—like the birth of a child or becoming the first female head pastor of
a church—make the preacher cognizant of her gender. The crucial criteria
came in feeling confident about their voice. Rev. Williams said, "I wouldn't
say that I'm really glad that I have a woman's voice to preach with. I would
simply say, I'm really glad God has called me to preach."

Gestures: Talking with the Hands and Intentional Theater

Explorations around the voice reveal how naturalness in preaching is, in
actuality, formed over time through the influences of culture, gender, and
religious tradition. A preacher's development of her voice occurs through
that spectrum of physicality, community, and personal choice. When the
topic turns to gestures, a similar scenario emerges. The women of this study
inherited a gestural system shaped by male bodies and an expectation that
they employ movement with ease. But when asked, women professed a
lack of intentionality concerning their gestures prior to preaching and little
awareness of them while speaking. "I don't practice my delivery," reported
Rev. Williams. "I probably ought to, but I don't." "I am not so aware of my
body," said Rev. Martin. She was surprised when a congregant approached
her after worship to comment on a gesture. "Really?" she said, "I kicked
my leg in the air. Really?" Others expressed some anxiety around pulpit

53. See Florence, *Preaching as Testimony*; Ziel, "Mother Tongue"; Hartman, "Feminist
Norms"; Tisdale, "Women's Ways of Communicating."

actions. Rev. Robinson reflected, "I'm trying to be more comfortable with gestures, although I'm not really clear what I'm doing." Only a few women could describe an instance when they utilized a gesture while preaching. Collectively, their approach appeared to be a largely unthinking one, a mixture of hoping to make use of their bodies coupled with no concrete plan of action. At first glance, then, a minimal approach to gestures presented as the most natural course of action. And yet their reticence around the topic, along with the legacy of gendered gestures, indicated there was more to be explored.

Broadly defined, a gesture is any movement of any part of the body that conveys a preacher's thought or emotion in order to reinforce oral expression.[54] Like the voice, gestures are bound by one's physical form while simultaneously working to extend a sermon through the body's involvement. Gestures can be classified as providing either descriptive or emphatic support.[55] One might trace an outline of the earth to depict God's all-encompassing love. One could raise her arms to heaven to emphasize a key point. Merleau-Ponty affirms that the meaning of a gesture is developed collaboratively between the one who gestures and the ones who receives the movement. As such, a gesture requires "a certain structural co-ordination of experience."[56] Performance theories add to these insights the aspiration that gestures flow naturally from the preacher's embodied awareness of her homiletical intent, as well as her passion for her subject.

When asked about their gestures, women acknowledged the positive role gestures play in preaching, even as they confessed some confusion about the particular acts they employed. Rev. Anderson affirmed that she used her body when she preached. She said, "I get excited. Sometimes I feel like I am fussing and, of course, gestures come with that. I am not fussing. I'm passionate." Having articulated her desire for greater comfort with movement, Rev. Robinson dreamt of having a feedback session with preaching mentors, who might be willing to point out how she tapped with her fingers or rocked side-to-side. In contrast, Rev. Walker intentionally planned her gestures. She said, "I am aware of my body when I preach. I

54. Farley states, "The movements and gestures made during a sermon should be full of meaning and purpose, directly related to the sermon itself, not to the comfort of the speaker" (121).

55. Ward, *Speaking of the Holy*, 36. He cites Don Wardlaw as delineating between emphatic gestures that make a point and descriptive gestures that make a picture. See also Kemper, *Effective Preaching*, 127.

56. Merleau-Ponty, *Phenomenology of Perception*, 225.

do work on my gestures and have little notes to myself in there [the manuscript]." She was one of the few women who recounted a time when she had utilized a gesture while preaching. The majority of women grew silent when the topic was introduced. Like Ms. Clark's self-report of not feeling embodied while she preached, they shied away from gestural conversations.

Multiple factors could contribute to the women's reticence. Their hesitation might represent the continuing power of male preaching models or the legacy of staged preaching poses, as earlier eras still cast a shadow. Or the women may stand in a paradoxical landscape in which intentional, explicit gestures are a skill set they recognize as valuable but have not yet developed. Whatever the roots, the general lack of engagement is noteworthy. Young's reference to the ways women may not make full use of their body's range of motion or embodied strength and the resultant timidity about their overall presence reemerges as worthy of consideration.[57] By not utilizing gestures women risk appearing as if their preaching embodiments are constrained. The door opens to evaluations about whether they have brought a sermon to completion or brought a sermon fully to life.

Despite their overall timidity in discussing gestures, women were not quiet in one important way. When asked about their gestures, women often responded with comments about their hands. Rev. Williams credited her love of preaching to another female preacher. After naming the woman's dynamic delivery, Rev. Williams concluded, "She talked a lot with her hands." Rev Harris also said, "I know I talk with my hands." Naming her desire to have a "whole body performance," Rev. Baker focused on her gestures, saying, "I speak with my hands a lot." Hands are involved in many gestures. Yet the women's responses framed their hand movements as somehow distinct from other commonly defined and recognizable preaching gestures. They further identified such hand talk as natural to them, a series of movements happening with ease. For many, their natural performance included talking with the hands.

When Ms. Clark began her sermon, her hands were clasped together and held at waist level in front of her body. She parted her hands and motioned toward the congregation as she spoke the opening sentences, as if to communicate "welcome." Shifting her hands to be parallel with one another in front of her body, she moved them up and down during the sermon's first movement, increasing her speed as she approached her section's climatic end. As she transitioned to another section of the sermon, she clasped her

57. Young, "Throwing like a Girl."

hands together again, allowing a second, similar pattern of gestures to un-
fold. Her hand movements continued throughout her sermon, a method of
preaching with her hands. Within gesture studies, such motions are termed
"beats" and understood to be relatively abstract movements whose focus
is on the structure rather than the content of the discourse.[58] Through her
hands, Ms. Clark provided a map of the sermon and revealed her connection to various moments in her proclamation.

These hand motions are gestures, experienced by many women as a
natural avenue for preaching embodiment. Their inclinations to bring form
to their sermons were filtered through the hands. Speaking of her hands,
Rev. Sarah Lockhart reflected, "It is almost like I cannot express a thought
without showing you. What I am communicating is so much that it comes
out from more than just my voice." At the same time, by using their hands
women gravitated to smaller, more contained bodily movements. Their
choices harkened to the type of female bodily constriction already named,
the impact of social constraints placed upon female bodies. In this way,
talking with the hands demonstrated, yet again, how culture shapes what
gestures fit what bodies. Hands motions, operating as beats, manifest the
overall structure of a sermon. In a related fashion, talking with their hands
revealed a woman's embodied relationship to her proclamation and a sense
of her place amid the preaching performance landscape. By gravitating to
the hands, women expressed a perception that larger or culturally authorized gestures are not as available or applicable to their bodies. Less comfortable with such movements, they nevertheless found an alternate way to
embody their words and perform a sermon.

Alongside the instances of talking with the hands, two preachers described moments when they employed actions that would fall under the
umbrella of more conventionally understood gestures. In both instances
the preachers' gestures further called into question the assumptions operating within the natural preaching performance schema. Rev. Harris deliberately blocked out her sermon positions. Rev. Walker dug into her bag
of cultural tropes to bring home her message. Their use of gestures added
another layer of critique upon the natural preacher ideal.

Drawing from her college experiences with theater, Rev. Harris translated stage directions into a practice for utilizing multiple points on the
sanctuary floor from which to preach. She chose different places on the

58. McNeill elaborates, "Beats look like beating musical time. The hands move along
with the rhythmical pulsation of speech" (*Hand and Mind*, 15).

floor depending upon the content and aim of each part of the sermon. For example, she stood at the base of the chancel steps, she said, "when I need to back up because this is a teaching moment. I'm doing the exegesis of the scripture. I'm talking to everyone." As she journeyed deeper into the sermon, she moved down into the aisle near the pews. She continued, "I really want to get in there with the congregation. I come down closer to you because this is the life application part of the sermon. This is the message I want you to take home with you." Although not speaking of gestures in their customary definition, Rev. Harris's body acted as its own gesture. Her diverse points for preaching enlivened the sermon. Rather than a "natural" gesture by virtue of lacking in self-consciousness, her gesture was planned. Simultaneously, it was a natural outgrown of her preaching intentions. It was a sincere movement, consistent with her personality, emotions, and the aims of her sermon. Using her theater skills authentically, she problematized the notion of natural in preaching.[59]

Rev. Walker also brought the dilemma between natural and unnatural gestures into stark relief. Having said she notes possible gestures in her sermon manuscript, she continued,

> I am a woman preacher, a black one and a Southern one. I'm also a mother. I don't mind stopping and shaking my finger and putting my hand on my hip. A man can't get away with that. A black woman preacher can do that. She can just stop and put her hand on her hip and say, "Oh come on, folks." And it is intentional theater because they know what I'm indicating in that moment.

As a single action used to emphasize her point, her hand on the hip broke open the distinctions between natural and unnatural movements, between sincerity and artifice. It was a self-consciously dramatic action, false in the sense of being borrowed as a cultural character exaggeration and yet utterly true in its use for homiletical effect. The emphasis upon a preacher's natural performance developed among public concerns about deception. A preacher whose actions were contrived might be engaging in inauthentic or hypocritical preaching. In this instance, Rev. Walker relied upon a contrived gesture not to deceive but to convey a message she believes with great sincerity. Not only was she acting, but she knew she was acting and

---

59. It is important to note that Childers seeks to correct the negative associations with performance and the unreflective use of natural with her notion of honest or truthful performance, which makes use of the insights of theater for the sake of enlivened preaching. See Childers, *Performing the Word*.

her listeners knew it as well. Such a performance was intentional artifice. But the artifice was not arbitrary. Rev. Walker identified herself as a black, Southern, female preacher. She used a gesture that has deep roots and expressive power in her context. However planned the gesture, it was used sincerely. Rev. Walker employed her body for the sake of bringing the sermon to completion. In doing so, she blurred the line between natural and unnatural gestures, revealing the limitations of defining natural as a single, precise style and of relying upon natural as the sole indicator of sincerity. Rev. Walker's decision reinforced how natural is a cultural creation; a performance repeated over time to appear natural and for some preachers, may even come to feel natural. The naturalness, though, is restricted to the embodied selves who have taken up the necessary set of repetitive actions with ease and complicity.

Natural, in its present conception, is limited. It is a compilation of movements tailored to certain bodies, which slowly became ingrained over years of habitual practices as preachers passed down gestures one to another. Absent a deep analysis of natural as a constructed category, it is too simplistic to instruct preachers to move naturally. Such advice minimizes the historical, cultural, and gender influences that have resulted in some bodies being more readily acceptable as natural bodies in the pulpit than others. The use of artifice reminds preachers and teachers of preaching that all preaching possesses some level of intentional theater. The ideals of congruence and consistency between preacher and preached sermon are worth preserving. It is valuable to evaluate a preacher's sincerity, to weigh in on the passions that compel one to preach. The expectation for a sermon to come to life through body and voice is a goal worth keeping as well. But congruence, consistency, and embodied performances can be retained without maintaining naturalness as their crucial indicator.

Performance Reconsidered: Agency, Sincerity, and Embodied Life

This chapter has concentrated upon the ways performance approaches to preaching have fallen short for a small selection of female preachers. While affirming that every preacher does perform, it argues that the ideology surrounding a natural performance has prevented the full performance of many women, who encounter a close link between male bodies and standards of performance. The task of performing a sermon—rather than simply writing a manuscript—is a task requiring diligent labor and no small measure of courage. Female preachers contend with concerns and comments about the distractive effects of clothes or adornments. They enter a space and a task that, until recently, barred their bodies from participating. To place their bodies in service of proclamation can be a loaded, risky endeavor. Any instructions to "be natural" in their performance clashes with the crowded, contradictory preaching space they now occupy.

The ideal of a natural performance presents itself as ahistorical. In reality, naturalness has formed steadily over time to be identified through certain gestures and vocal inflections. Because naturalness developed within a social context, the markers of natural are products of a culture, and specifically gendered embodiments born from the assumed male preacher. When female preachers attempted to respond to the expectations of a natural performance and imitate these male forms, they experienced a split between the kinds of preaching performances that came naturally to them and the preaching roles they were expected to assume. To heal the rupture necessitated laying aside the prevailing natural ideal. They borrowed skills from the theater. They talked with their hands. They claimed the materiality of their voices. All of these strategies illumined the women's agency. And purposeful agency carried with it sincerity. As Rev. Walker's example demonstrated, intentional theater can be deeply sincere. Mrs. Clark's movement of her hands symbolized how her body stayed alert and attuned to her sermon. While naturalness as it stands is a criterion in need of correction, sincerity is a critical aspect of a preacher's performance and a criterion worth preserving.

In his work on performance, Richard F. Ward concludes, "The aim of a performance-perspective in preaching is not to aggravate the preacher by aiming a spotlight at his or her vocal or physical agility, but it is for deepening our understanding of why we preach at all."[60] We preach, suggests Ward, in order to bring into the sacred conversation those who have dwelled for too long on the margins. Ward writes, as "in performance a human being reveals self to self," the sermon provides a way "that the selfhood of both preachers and listeners are reconstituted during the preaching event."[61] A preacher brings herself to the sermon, a self formed and still forming via her physicality, culture, and choices. Her experiences of preaching enable the reconstitution of performance, which, in turn, aids the preacher and listener to more readily meet each other amid the proclaimed word. It is in

60. Ward, "Performance Turns in Homiletics," para. 38.
61. Ibid., para. 21 and 38.

this sense that a preacher serves as an instrument of God's presence, offering her performing self, oriented to God and other. Rev. Harris decided one Sunday to use a ladder to illustrate the people who support our climbs of faith. Sitting in the pew before the sermon, she panicked. "How am I going to climb this ladder with this manuscript in my hand?" she thought. "And it was like the voice of God said to me, 'You wrote this. Just get up there and preach it.'" In risking her particularly crafted performance, Rev. Harris discovered the power of embodiment and how her living body makes possible the revealing of self to self and selves in front of God.

CHAPTER 6

Preaching Pregnant

Following the spring of her graduation from seminary and ordination in the United Methodist Church, the Reverend Erica Williams received an appointment to her first church, a solid, healthy, rural congregation. She married her college sweetheart a few weeks after graduation, entering ministry and marriage in the same season. The church had a history of female pastors. They welcomed her wholeheartedly, quickly responding to her frank yet easygoing style. Initially, the main reactions to her presence focused upon her age. Rev. Williams was in her mid-twenties, making her the youngest minister ever to serve the church. "I have been really honest with people about my age," remarked Rev. Williams. "I know that I'm young." When a congregant said to her "I've never had a minister young enough to be my granddaughter," Rev. Williams laughingly replied, "If it would make you feel better, I can call you grandma." Her non-defensive, open nature won her many admirers. So did her preaching. Viewing the preaching space as "a very holy place to be," Rev. Williams removed her shoes when she began, gravitated toward a style that "lingers in the text," and comfortably shifted from pulpit to sanctuary floor. Finding her sermons well received, she gained confidence in crafting ones she hoped would both comfort and challenge her congregation.

Whether it was her age or her newly married status, Rev. Williams frequently fielded questions about pregnancy. "Almost since day one of being here, I've had people routinely ask me whether or not I'm pregnant," she said, "or when I'm planning on having children." If she held a baby in front of the congregation during a baptism, inevitably someone commented,

"You're looking mighty comfortable there. Are you thinking about start-ing a family?" If she remarked around the office, "I could really go for a hamburger right now," someone asked, "Are you sure you're not pregnant?" Sometimes the inquiry came entirely unbidden. Church members stopped her in a hallway to say, "I hope you don't mind me asking, but are you expecting?" Although recognizing the questions arose from her public role and her status as a married woman of childbearing years, the persistency of the questions disturbed her. "I am very comfortable with my body," Rev. Williams reflected, "but it would give me a complex if I took seriously the amount of times people have asked me that question." As the months passed and the questions continued, she found herself dressing in form-fitting clothes that avoided a loose, flowing look. She also thought carefully about the subtext embedded in the questions and their relationship to her developing identity as a female preacher.

Rev. Williams's primary objection to questions about pregnancy lay in their intimate nature. She pondered over "the information people think they have a right to know about you as a pastor," including information about one's sexual behavior. "Do you realize," she remarked, "that basically you are asking me if I've had unprotected sex with my husband?" Although acknowledging that most parishioners were probably "just thinking 'we want to play with a baby,'" the intrusiveness of the questions transgressed the professional boundary she desired to set between herself and the con-gregation. At the same time, she recognized the questions could be viewed as well-meaning attempts to forge a connection with her. "I think it is a way to relate to me," she said, "because I am so much younger than them. And while they accept me as a pastor, with that authority and role, I think it is challenging for them to really understand how to relate to me interperson-ally." Eventually she took such questions as an opportunity to establish her role. "I usually say, for the record, no, I'm not pregnant. For future ref-erence, that is not an appropriate question to ask somebody because you never know what they are going through. They could be having trouble conceiving or they may just have had a miscarriage or they are pregnant and they aren't ready to tell people."

The topic of pregnancy came up often during Rev. Williams's initial interview, as questions about preaching, bodies, theology, and ministry seemed to circle back to questions about being pregnant. What I, as the interviewer, did not know at that time was that Rev. Williams was newly pregnant. About six weeks along, she chose not to divulge the information even as pregnancy—and being a pregnant preacher—served as the focus of the interview. Fourteen months later, we met again. During the second interview, Rev. Williams spoke at length about an early miscarriage, her second pregnancy that led to the birth of a son, and the impact of these experiences on her preaching life. In this conversation, the issue of boundaries came into sharper focus as she enumerated what information she shared with her congregation, what she kept private, how she navigated the physical changes of her body as a public figure, and how she handled boundaries that expanded by necessity. The processes of pregnancy, miscarriage, and childbirth were intensely physical experiences. They called upon her internal resources, her theological worldview, and her flexibility in relating to her congregation. Ultimately these experiences raised questions about how embodied life impacts proclamation.

When asked to describe her theology of the body in her first interview, Rev. Williams said confidently, "The body has value, worth, and purpose, otherwise Jesus wouldn't have taken one on. But I don't believe the body is all of our identity either. It is only a piece of who we are." A year later, after listening to her description of having a "lovable alien in her belly," I asked Rev. Williams if her perspective on the body had changed. She answered, "No, not substantially. I do still think that our bodies are very much a part of who we are but at the same time they don't define us. We are more than just our bodies." She named pregnancy, a time when her body felt out of her control, as a period that strained her belief in the body's partial role in forming identity. Food cravings, weight gains, and the baby's movements kept her acutely attuned to her body. Her growing belly forced her to modify her activities and remember she was sharing bodily space with someone else. Yet even within this tension she maintained, "the fundamental core of who I was hasn't changed, even as my body was so different than what it was."

Pregnant Embodiment: A Doubling

In her work "Pregnant Embodiment," Iris Marion Young argues, "The pregnant subject . . . is decentered, split, or doubled in several ways."[1] As the pregnant woman's bodily self-location becomes "focused on her trunk in addition to her head" and the body's "inner movements belong to another being, even as they are not other," the pregnant woman "experiences her

---

1. Young, "Pregnant Embodiment," 46.

body as herself and not herself."² Akin to Rev. William's language about carrying a "lovable alien," Young suggests that the process of hosting another body makes fluid the boundary "between what is within, myself, and what is outside, separate."³ She writes, "I experience my insides as the space of another, yet my own body."⁴ Living within this fluidity of boundaries, the pregnant woman splits into two modes of being. She is her former body, often using pre-pregnant forms of movement. She is also a different, new body, discovering that she has less balance, more weight, and moves in heavier, less spontaneous ways. These physical changes, and especially the doubling of the body, challenge the assumption of a self as always and everywhere unified.⁵ The pregnant woman attends to both herself and her baby. Her materiality is simultaneously her old body and a new body just as her physicality contains both her former body and the developing fetus. Thus pregnancy reveals how "the unity of the self is itself a project, a project sometimes successfully enacted by a moving and often contradictory subjectivity."⁶

In her recollections of pregnancy, Rev. Williams articulated the tension that arose as her body hosted another life. The changes wrought by her growing child made her aware that her body felt less like her possession. Simultaneously, she strongly affirmed that the core of who she was had not changed. The unity of the self was a project during her pregnancy, as she held the contradictions of a changing body and a continuous self. With so much attention focused on the physically quantifiable aspects of pregnancy, the pregnant woman may wonder, "Am I just my body?" or "Am I only my body?" These questions are particularly poignant when one's body feels less and less her own. And such questions prompt reflection upon the persistent separation of mind and body, with identity being located in the mind. As the locus of attention turns from head to trunk, the pregnant woman encounters how physical changes impact identity, even if the changes do not alter it entirely. A self that is a project, and sometimes a contradictory project, can hold the paradox of "I am my body and I am more than it also."

2. Ibid.

3. Ibid., 49.

4. Ibid.

5. Young writes, "Pregnancy, I argue, reveals a paradigm of bodily experience in which the transparent unity of self dissolves and the body attends positively to itself at the same time that it enacts its projects" (ibid., 47).

6. Ibid., 48.

Preaching Pregnant: Finding the Boundaries

Pregnancy and childbirth call upon the body in specific and profound ways. Over the course of forty weeks, the entire body expands as blood volume doubles, the belly grows, and everything from feet, hands, and face grow in concert. The pregnant preacher contends with these bodily changes while she preaches. With her belly extending, she may find her balance skewed, her energy diminished, and her lungs incapable of holding their normal capacity of air. As the body "weighs into" the sermon in a new way, the pregnant preacher encounters an ever-watchful congregation. Many will comment freely about her body's changes or routinely ask her how she feels. Preachers can experience the congregation's perceived ownership over their bodies, just as a baby stakes his or her claim. Young conceives of the pregnant body as doubling or splitting, naming well the blurring boundaries that occur between mother and baby, inside and outside, self and other. But within this small group of preachers, the experiences of pregnant embodiment involved tackling the project of the self—not necessarily a unified self or a self devoid of contradictions—by marking their boundaries with greater clarity, precision, and confidence. Pregnancy became a time when they learned the limits of what they would share publicly and what they would not, when they established firmer lines between their embodied lives and their congregations, and when they recognized how their evolving embodiment intersected with their preaching.

Rev. Williams was one of several preachers in this study who combined child bearing with preaching. Four of those preachers, Rev. Harris, Rabbi Levin, Rev. Lockhart, and Rev. Williams, spoke in detail about being a pregnant preacher. This chapter will explore how these four women navigated the task of preaching while pregnant, in hopes of drawing broader insights into how the ever-developing, embodied self informs preaching. Pregnancy is a decidedly female experience. Pregnancy can intrude upon the female preachers who aren't pregnant, as they also may deflect questions about pregnancy or manage their bodies to minimize such inquiries. Furthermore, pregnancy brings into sharper relief the commonly shared experience among female preachers of having their bodies closely observed. The preachers in this study routinely commented that "it is as if my body is not my own" during interview subjects ranging from shoes, hairstyles, or clothes to unsolicited advice about preaching postures. Since both the congregation and the growing fetus fostered such thoughts, exploring how the pregnant preacher reasserted some ownership of her body offers insights into embodied reclamation in multiple dimensions of preaching. By charting the key stories shared around pregnancy in preaching, the complex, ever-evolving, and at times elusive, embodied sense of the self becomes more visible. Successful efforts to stake a claim on one's identity also come into sharper focus. If it is true that "without bodies preaching is not worth talking about," then the pregnant preacher's experience of her body and her efforts to create more life-giving space—for baby, herself, and her sermon—are vital to understanding the unfolding project of preaching as well.[7]

Preaching through Miscarriage

Before they could talk about pregnancies, women told stories about their miscarriages. Two women suffered the heartache of preaching amid a pregnancy loss. Their histories reflected how miscarriage and pregnancy do go together, with one in four pregnancies ending in miscarriage.[8] As is often the case, the women had not publicly shared the news of their pregnancy when they lost the baby. Consequently, they found themselves preaching amid an atmosphere of silent knowing, attempting to bring a sermon to birth while their bodies were shedding a life. Faced with holding their grief while delivering a sermon, Rev. Harris and Rev. Lockhart spoke of separating what was happening in their bodies from their preaching.

Rev. Harris miscarried on Christmas Eve. "I was standing in the pulpit, preaching about babies," she recounted "and I was bleeding. I knew something was wrong, and that was really hard. It was one of the few times I had to really disconnect my body, my physical embodiment from the words I was preaching." Normally a preacher keenly aware of and situated in her body, Rev. Harris used starkly different language to talk about her experience that evening. Faced with an achingly painful night in which to miscarry, she set aside blood, fear, and sadness in hopes of embodying babies, birth, and joy. In such a situation, she made the necessary and wise choice to block out, temporarily, one embodied event in order to perform another one.

It was the middle of Lent when the Reverend Lockhart learned that she was pregnant, after trying for several months to conceive. "I found out that I was pregnant in March," she said "and in April of Holy Week, I had a

7. Childers, "Preacher's Body," 224.

8. Barrett, *What Was Lost*, xiii.

miscarriage. I had gone for a sonogram earlier because I had had a little bit of bleeding. There was a heart rate but it wasn't really fast enough. When I went back two weeks later, it was gone." Devastated, Rev. Lockhart was scheduled to preach in two days. "So the next Sunday, I had to preach a Palm Sunday sermon," she continued. "It was a really good sermon and I remember feeling like normally preaching is one of those things that takes from me, in a really good way. It is one of those 'this is me' types of moments. And in that situation I felt like I was able to do it and there was nothing of me that I was really giving." Having to shepherd the congregation during the central week of the Christian year, Rev. Lockhart also framed her experience with words of disconnection. What was typically a "this is me" type moment became a space where "there was nothing of me" to give.

Rev. Harris and Rev. Lockhart described situations in which they preached through death and all the shock, sorrow, and pain such loss evokes. Countless preachers have preached through crisis: approaching the pulpit as they await results for a biopsy, manage a family emergency, or while going through a divorce. What distinguishes these two preachers' experiences is the proximity of birth and death happening in their bodies. On a material level there was no separation between the processes of miscarriage and the actions of standing, speaking, and moving to preach. The women evoked the language of separation to describe how they moved through the moment. They made space between the internal events of their body and the occasion of their preaching. They preached "without anything of me" in the sermon. Their language illuminates how the mind-body split remains operative, such that it is possible to conceive of having "disconnected one's body from one's words." In reality, the mind is never separated from the body, the body is always present in one's preaching, and the body and the mind are constantly responding to one another. Within this fragile unity, though, Rev. Harris and Rev. Lockhart attempted to convey the agonizing moments that force a separation between mother and preacher, between public preacher and private self. Their experiences unveil how deeply the events of our lives—the things that happen in, through, and with our bodies—impact our whole selves. They inescapably shape not just what we preach but how we preach. Without embodied life we, and those who listen to us, might well say, "There was nothing of the preacher in that sermon."

While extreme, preaching through miscarriage represents the shared experiences of many preachers who temporarily suspend something in order to concentrate on a sermon. Such moments shatter the illusion of a fully unified self.[9] When one feels shattered in the pulpit, torn into pieces by life, one becomes attuned to the diverse elements that make up the self, with each element placing a demand upon the sermon. In these moments, the vitality possible in embodiment is present in its absence. The self does not feel coherent. The painful, harder-to-integrate experiences evoke a sense of disembodied preaching, even as the preaching moment becomes a moment to remember the self.

Young suggests the recognition of the illusion of a unified self prompts a reconfiguration of the embodied self. The doubling process of pregnancy ultimately empowers the pregnant woman to attend simultaneously to her body and the growing fetus. She is not expected to make these two things one, although the mother and the baby coexist in the same space. Her task is to hold them in a paradoxical harmony, sometimes easily in sync and sometimes painfully at odds. In corresponding ways, the "me" that is potently possible in preaching is never a perfectly formed, internally reconciled, static self. It is the "me" of contradiction, paradox, and uneasy growth.

Two weeks later, Rev. Lockhart preached again. Having survived Holy Week, in which reading Jesus' words to his mother Mary standing at the foot of the cross required enormous effort, she poured herself into a resurrection sermon.

> I preached the Sunday after Easter and I started crying during my sermon. It was something about believing in the Resurrection, that I believe in resurrection. I never said what I was talking about and so people could have thought that I had just gotten emotional. But I remember feeling how cathartic it felt to write it. It was the first real thing I had written about it [the miscarriage]. It felt—not like it was healed—but that it was healing to preach it. *Yeah, it felt like me again.* (emphasis mine)

Your Preacher Is Pregnant: Sharing the News

Dealing with a miscarriage while preaching raised questions about the ways embodiment impacted and, conversely, could be separated from, preaching. Since miscarriages tended to remain private, the questions also remained somewhat private. The questions shifted, though, when a

9. Young, "Pregnant Embodiment," 48. Young is challenging Merleau-Ponty and others who hold to a unified self.

pregnancy proceeded as hoped. Upon learning they were pregnant, most preachers kept the news initially within a small circle of close connections. But as they approached the twelve-week mark, when the risk of miscarriage diminished significantly and their bodies started showing its pregnant state, women faced decisions about announcing the pregnancy to a congregation. Their decision-making processes focused on framing the message in a manner that not only shared the joyous news but also affirmed their pastoral identity. Announcing the pregnancy generated much thoughtful preplanning, as a key moment when private news moved into the public domain. The means by which they announced their pregnancy became the method by which they guided their congregations in relating to a pregnant preacher. The dilemma of the self became organized around holding two identities, mother-to-be and preacher, in a loose, shifting manner that both reached out to the congregation and created limits in the congregation's involvement in the pregnancy.

When she was expecting her first child, Rev. Harris chose Mother's Day to tell her church. Utilizing the community's tradition of giving flowers to mothers during worship, she paused when the time came to distribute the flowers and said, "Oh, I guess that includes me." When she was pregnant with her second child, she also folded the announcement into Sunday worship. During the sharing of joys and concerns before the congregational prayer, she said, "It is so wonderful to have all these kids here and we're just so excited about how much our church is growing. So Peter and I have decided we want to contribute to this growth." In both instances, Rev. Harris used annual events to offer relatively brief, upbeat messages about the coming baby. She intentionally drew upon congregational rites, seeking to fit the pregnancy into the church's ongoing life. "I wanted to put it in that context," she said, "and have people see me in that moment as both pastor and as mother, that I'm wearing these two hats." By blending the news with church news, she remained firmly within her role as pastor even as she touched upon her role as a mother. She created a framework for how the congregation would relate to her. They would share in her pregnancy but she was primarily their pastor.

Now faced with sharing the news of another baby on the way, Rev. Harris admitted to feeling self-conscious each time she approached these announcements. Speeches about pregnancies heightened the attention directed toward her and especially toward her physical appearance. "My body is going to change," she continued. "The thing I was really aware of when I was pregnant with Sidney was how much more quickly I showed, and how by the time I was comfortable announcing it at church, it was fairly obvious." By keeping the announcement short and within the secure container of a liturgical moment, she hoped to decrease some of the intense observations. She recognized her efforts would meet limited success. Rev. Harris had waited well into the second trimester to share the news of her coming second child, delaying the announcement because of her earlier miscarriage. Afterward several parishioners remarked, "We knew [you were pregnant]. We could tell." "It was strange," commented Rev. Harris, "to think that people had been watching and looking at my body and making assumptions." With this most recent occasion, she has debated not making a formal announcement. "I've considered just telling the leadership team and small groups of people and letting the word get out," she said. Thinking it might be fun to see what happened, she has wondered what it would be like to have "people just ask me, so are you pregnant?" Although fairly certain she will share the news more formally in worship, she's equally aware of the appeal embedded in avoiding an announcement altogether.

While the interview conversations about these decisions were often light-hearted, the moment of saying publicly "I am pregnant" was a deeply serious matter for the women. Those who had lost a pregnancy felt the risks associated with sharing the news. Each preacher remembered she was addressing her congregation, which made the announcement a formal moment with workplace implications. Choosing to speak as the first trimester faded into the second, the announcement itself became a hinge point in their experiences as pregnant preachers. It marked the transition when what had been a largely internal event starts becoming externally visible. From a different analytical lens, these women announced their pregnancies just as the boundaries of their bodies started to become truly fluid. During the second trimester, a woman will feel the baby move, her belly will noticeably swell, and she will really need maternity clothes. Her body's boundaries—between mother and children, self and world—recede as the growing baby increasingly takes up space and the mother's expanding belly pushes out into the world. As her body's boundaries diminished, Rev. Harris found ways to remain the preacher-pastor. She stayed in her preacher role as she introduced a pregnancy. Her announcement affirmed her professional identity and attempted to create a fluid yet firm boundary between her pregnancy and her preaching.

Another preacher, also concerned about boundaries, used her announcement to communicate specific expectations with her congregation. She, in fact, drew a line around her body through the medium of sharing the news. When describing her pregnancy announcement, Rev. Williams began with a prior experience. "My husband and I have over the course of the last year lost some weight," she explained.

> When I first started losing weight, I would have old ladies in the receiving line [after worship] put their hands on my hips and say, "You look so good." They would have a hand on my butt. And I'd be [thinking], "Wow, you really just felt me up there." It was clear they did not understand my body was my own and not their territory. I thought to myself if they feel that comfortable now, when I'm not pregnant, how much more so are they going to feel that way when I do get pregnant.

Prior even to conceiving, she knew she wanted to curtail the congregation's access to her body.

So when she came to share the news, Rev. Williams announced what she named as both a joy and a concern during the prayer time of Sunday morning worship. "The joy," she said, "is that Chris and I are expecting our first child." The congregation clapped and cheered. "But my concern," she continued, "is that I have this serious phobia of people touching my belly." As she expected, her congregation laughed. Then she said, "No, I'm serious, so serious that my friend made this t-shirt for me." She held up a shirt with a handprint marked through with a big X and a caption underneath that read "Hands off the belly." The congregation roared. She concluded, "So you can pray for the health of the baby and that when people touch my belly I can respond in a Christian way." She repeated her announcement at all morning services.

Rev. Williams used the announcement of her pregnancy to say far more than that she was expecting a child. She combined an unorthodox approach with humor to create a firm boundary between her pregnant body and her congregation's eagerness to touch. Her announcement revealed the vulnerabilities attached to the pregnant body. The pregnant preacher sensed the risks associated with the congregation's attention and possible touch. Acknowledging that people are drawn to pregnant bellies and encouraging the congregation's welcome of the coming child, Rev. Williams proclaimed what they could and could not do. The hands would stay off the belly. Her body (and her baby) would have space to grow.

Preaching as a Pregnant Body

Although creative in her communication method, Rev. Williams's desire to craft a boundary between her pregnancy and her church was a commonly shared goal. Announcing the pregnancy was the first step in the process. Maintaining enough space for the baby's and mother's growth was the next project. As women adjusted to growing bodies, the changes in their bodies changed their experience of preaching. They learned how to preach pregnant.

Young characterizes the pregnant body as the one aware of its fullness rather than its lack.[10] Moving away from assumptions that the added weight or corresponding cumbersomeness creates a gulf between a woman and her body, Young argues that pregnant embodiment encourages awareness of the body and an appreciation for the body's role "as the means to the accomplishment of my aims."[11] The pregnant body is a productive body, a body not defined by its capacity to distract nor minimized in its femininity, but powerfully embodied by the task of nurturing life. Young's reversal of lack into fullness resonated with this group of pregnant women. Their narratives illustrated her main proposal, demonstrating how living in and through a pregnant body grounds a woman, both in the solid materiality that is her body and in the potency of a growing fetus. While speaking frankly about the physical challenges and inconveniences associated with pregnancy, these women also told of discovering new strength.

The women recited a host of bodily discomforts that accompanied them through the nine months. When they walked toward the pulpit, they did so at a slower pace and with an unsteady balance. As they preached, they did so with aching backs and swollen feet. "It took more out of me physically to preach," reflected Rev. Lockhart. "Pregnancy was definitely a challenge," said Rabbi Levin. "I'm not a loud speaker anyway, and it took more effort to speak with more limited breath, less air space, and [because of her larger belly] farther away from the microphone." Rev. Harris remembered "getting so hot underneath her robe" and being momentarily distracted when the baby moved or kicked. The demands of a pregnant body could intersect with the requirements of preaching, sometimes in unanticipated or awkward ways. Rev. Lockhart struggled to make it through worship without needing to use the bathroom. She said, "A couple of times

10. Young, "Pregnant Embodiment," 51–53. See also Gadow, "Body and Self," 172–85.
11. Young, "Pregnant Embodiment," 51.

I had to pee in the service right before I was going to preach, and I thought 'what do I do?' Do I go and then they are going to be waiting for the sermon? I don't want everyone quiet and me walking back in from going to the bathroom." Keenly attuned of the body's needs, women wondered about the congregation's awareness of those same needs. Moving with obvious effort, speaking with less air, or having to rush to the bathroom strained their sense of bodily control or competency.

Pregnancy also affected the preacher's capacity for sustained concentration. Admitting she was a Saturday night sermon writer, Rev. Lockhart said, "It was harder to focus and write my sermon. Preparation-wise I was so exhausted and mentally all over the place." Rev. Harris recounted a time she lost her place during a sermon. A preacher who preaches without a manuscript, she remembered, "One time, I went completely blank. I had one of those pregnancy brain moments. I said 'I have no idea what I was going to say,' which made everyone laugh. Then I said, 'I hate pregnancy.' Everyone laughed again. It was a humorous moment and then I got back on track." Just as women adjusted to a different physicality, they faced compensating for altered mental capabilities. As the focus moved from "head to trunk," their preaching occasionally reflected the shift.

These bodily changes located women in two simultaneous tasks. They were preachers who were pregnant. One mode of interpretation suggests pregnancy imprisons women in their bodies as they become bound to their physical limitations.[12] Offering an alternative analysis, Young argues that the pregnant woman becomes exceptionally aware of her essential embodiment in a manner that affirms her "power, solidity, and validity.[13] In their ability to compensate mental lapses or less lung capacity, these women experienced the positive power of their bodies and their continued ability to preach.

Furthermore, women reported perceiving of their bodies differently while pregnant. They expanded the images they held about themselves and discovered neglected dimensions. In general, they were more aware of being women. Rev. Harris said, "It [the body] changes so much, so rapidly, and I feel so feminine. I feel like I'm so curvy, so busty." Pregnancy, she continued, "is such the fertility Goddess thing. I'm fairly flat chested but not in pregnancy, not when I'm nursing. You are glowing, [the] thick hair . . . the hormones make you feel all the more." Although a larger chest and curvy

12. See Longhurst, *Maternities*; Westfall, "Pregnant/Birthing Body."
13. Young, "Pregnant Embodiment," 53.

hips made her more self-conscious about her body, Rev. Harris also reveled in her body's powerful beauty. Rev. Williams, who did not care much about her clothes in pre-pregnancy days, noted "while I didn't drastically change my style, I did dress more feminine when I was pregnant. I'm not much of a dress person or a skirt person, but during the pregnancy I wore a fair amount of those. And wanted to, which I just found really fascinating." Rev. Williams could not explain why she shifted toward more explicitly feminine clothes yet remembered her instinctive gravitation toward them. The physical changes of pregnancy do accentuate breasts and, at least for some time, hips. Like the body's intrusion through backaches and swollen feet, these embodiments are difficult to dismiss. The physiological changes in pregnancy may work in tandem with the physical to enable access to elements of the self normally minimized. Whatever the reasons, pregnant embodiment resulted in a shift in the self for these two women. One felt more feminine. Another dressed in ways more associated with the feminine. And they characterized such femininity in positive terms. It was the "fertility Goddess thing."

The capacity of the body to shelter life may spark knowledge of the body's fullness. Over time the baby—this life that is a part of them and yet not them—contributed to the fullness as well. Rev. Williams's baby asserted his presence when she prepared or delivered a sermon. She recalled,

> Anytime I sat to write my sermon or was preaching my sermon, the baby moved almost the entire time. It was really distracting to have this baby doing summersaults. At first I thought it was a fluke, but it just kept happening. And so I told my husband, "I don't know if it is my energy level or emotional state of being, [but] I'm pretty sure I'm not imagining this." My husband looked at me and said, "What other baby do we know of that moved in the presence of Christ?"

The Pregnant Preacher and Her Congregation

The internal fullness female preachers experienced could be challenged by their outward interactions with their congregation. Eager parishioners could flood women with intrusive questions, unwanted attention, and unsolicited comments. Each woman reacted uniquely in such occasions, but in general they worked to maintain a boundary between personal and professional, pregnancy and preacher. The blurring of boundaries occurring within, between mother and child, was contrasted by outward efforts to create stronger boundaries between themselves and their congregations.

Once congregations were aware the preacher was pregnant, they maintained a steady interest in the unfolding pregnancy. They inquired about the woman's health. They noted weight gains or other physical changes. Rev. Lockhart began to expect the regular check-up questions while greeting worshippers at the sanctuary door each Sunday. She said, "I remember a friend saying how exhausting it got for people to ask 'how are you feeling?' every week for seven months." Upon hearing her cheerful "things are great" reply, some congregants moved on to her appearance. Rev. Lockhart was a tall, thin woman, whose growing belly was quite noticeable. She was frequently told she looked like Friar Tuck in her robe with the belt tied just below her belly. She said, "Every week someone would come up to me and make the same joke about where the belt was, as if I hadn't heard it already. Several people said 'if you get much bigger that robe isn't going to fit.' I remember thinking Wow. I'm okay with being pregnant and looking big but I'm not okay with people commenting on it." Reacting in a similar fashion to similar comments, Rev. Williams privately created a list of things people shouldn't say to a pregnant woman. The list included "You've looking plump these days" and "There she is eating again." "It is interesting," she reflected, "that people feel like they can say whatever they want when you are pregnant. For me, it was constant." Unsolicited remarks about the size of their bodies or the amount of food on their plates stirred discomfort in these preachers. Aware of their very public roles, women viewed the comments as tangible reminders of how intently others watched their bodies. Rabbi Levin also experienced "people mak[ing] comments about the size of my belly." She concluded that "having the body changes happen in front of a congregation," creates another situation in which congregations act "as though your body belongs to them."

None of these women articulated anxiety about their changing bodies. Perhaps attuned to its fullness, they emphasized the healthiness associated with proper weight gain and a well-balanced prenatal diet. Their disquiet stemmed from others' comments. When receiving a boundary-crossing remark, Rabbi Levin typically smiled and kept moving. She might note the mark internally and occasionally she drew a mental line between herself and the commenter. She rarely voiced her disquiet. In contrast, Rev. Lockhart considered herself a very public person. She enjoyed a free-flowing give and take with church members, many of whom she characterized as friends. She was surprised, then, by her reactions to congregants' inquiries about her pregnancy. When asked, "How are you feeling?" she rarely said anything beyond "All is well." She explained, "It was hard in this very public thing. People are constantly asking you about it. If I was feeling really anxious about something, I couldn't spill that on them." She consciously chose not to share her anxiety, while recognizing the uniqueness of that choice for her. She realized she didn't want to provide the private details of her pregnancy to her congregation. She concluded, "I am not as public as I think I am. I'm very open but there are limits to that, and I hadn't known them that much until this whole experience."

In addition to frequent comments and questions, parishioners touched the bellies of their pregnant preachers. Reaching out to feel the belly was an evocative action, one more intimate than noticing weight gains. Each woman had her own perspective on having her body touched. Rev. Harris said, "I'm a fairly touchy person. I hug people all the time at church. It depended for me on who it was, what the context was. If it was someone I felt comfortable with, then I didn't mind. I've touched other pregnant women's bellies. It is a really cool thing. I can see why people would want to do it." As long as she was in the right space, Rev. Harris welcomed sharing her pregnant embodiment with others. Rabbi Levin was a more private person. Acutely conscious of the multiple times she felt inappropriately touched, she said, "I definitely remember having this feeling that my personal space had been invaded. Again, I was public property." Occasionally she would ask someone not to touch her. But typically she would walk away while silently protesting, "This is my body. It does not belong to the entire congregation." Rev. Williams had drawn a strong line around her belly prior to its most prominent growth. She expected that her request would decrease the number of times she was touched, but not eliminate the touching all together. She was pleasantly surprised when "not a single person in this congregation touched my belly without first asking me." The preestablished belly boundary further strengthened her ability to interact with congregants who struggled with her request. "I had one woman who came up to me and said, 'I'm going to touch your belly yet,'" she elaborated. "And her husband goes, 'I keep telling her not to.' And I said 'Resist the urge, resist.' And so we all laughed and she walked away and it was fine."

Young's work on pregnancy focused upon the processes occurring within a woman's body. Her argument is largely an internal one. Notions of doubling or splitting relate to the pregnant body's expansion, as two lives share one house. From this perspective, pregnant embodiment is characterized by a fluidity of boundaries. The strength of Young's argument lies in its reclamation of the body's resourcefulness. By reorienting the body's boundaries, she promotes a pregnant woman's lived awareness of her embodied strength and potential. In contrast, the preachers of this study were public figures constantly interacting with congregations highly invested in their doubling bodies. The process of preaching pregnant stretched the already thin boundaries between parishioners and pastors. Invited into an intensely personal and physically focused nine months, congregations could enact that invitation by being inappropriately inquisitive and intrusively demonstrative. Such behaviors are socially sanctioned and replicated far beyond the domain of female preachers and their churches. These women responded by establishing boundaries. They put a line over their belly, saying clearly "Do Not Touch." They answered, "All is well," even when anxious about a test or procedure. Like every aspect of embodied life, they felt their way through being pregnant, negotiating with the congregation as the months unfolded. However the boundaries came to be, what was internally fluid became externally firm.

Preaching about Pregnancy

Among their boundary-establishing decisions, women faced choices about whether or not to bring their pregnancies into their sermons. While they sometimes referred to their pregnancies in passing ways, they rarely decided to incorporate their pregnancies in any meaningful form into the sermon's content. Given the rich descriptions they had offered about being pregnant, their silence in the pulpit stands out. Such silence might be interpreted in several ways. It may be that the scriptures for the sermons didn't lend themselves to pregnancy illustrations. It may be that other themes or needs of the congregation took precedence in sermon planning. I would argue that the silence continues the boundary decisions already made. Women carved out a space in which their pregnancies took a supporting role to the primary task of preaching. They were still very much pregnant as they preached—even liturgical robes could not hide their growing bodies—but by not explicitly mentioning their pregnancies or their soon-to-be-born children they asserted another set of limits.

When the interview topic turned to preaching about pregnancy, women first named their hesitation. Each remembered those in the pews who longed for a child or grieved the loss of a baby. Pastoral sensitivities, it seemed, dissuaded them from drawing explicit attention to the emergent life. Alongside a desire to protect listeners from undue pain, women wanted to avoid anything that might encourage the congregation's attention to the pregnancy. Pregnancy, said Rev. Harris, "is very personal, very physical experience and I was not sure I wanted to talk about it in a public way." Rabbi Levin echoed her sentiments. "While I definitely used my pregnancy as a prop," she said, "making slight references to it or a joke in passing, I never wanted to get very personal." The personal dimension of pregnancy for both themselves and their listeners seemed at odds with the public nature of proclamation.

Occasionally an element in worship made it impossible not to refer to their pregnant status. Rev. Baker was preaching one Sunday when the epistle lesson came from 1 Timothy. She listened to a parishioner lead the congregation through words that included "women being saved through childbirth."[14] Eight months pregnant at the time, she then walked into the pulpit and said, "Well, I know I'm saved." Her sermon focused on the day's Gospel text. She reflected, "I made a joke about it. It was just too strange to preach on that [text] to women who might be childless or infertile. And I couldn't ignore it [the passage] because I was so obviously pregnant."

Rev. Harris was the only preacher who recalled a specific time in which she used her pregnancy in a sermon illustration. One December Sunday toward the end of her pregnancy, she compared her weekly doctor's appointments, in which the nurse checked her weight gain and the baby's position, to the measurements taken by those preparing spiritually for Christmas. Serving as the sermon's opening illustration, it felt appropriate to the season, personal without being exceedingly revealing, and ultimately contained within the sermon's larger purposes. Most significantly, Rev. Harris offered just one instance in which she included something about pregnancy in her preaching, despite having preached regularly over the course of multiple pregnancies.

Another preacher shared her experience. "I, too, was surprised that I didn't choose to preach on pregnancy too often," said Rev. Lockhart. "It wasn't just because it would get old. It was also that I needed some of it just to be for me and not for everyone to share. Again [it became] one of those places where I discovered the boundary. I didn't want to tell everyone everything that is going on." By not inserting pregnancy stories into their

14. 1 Tim 2:15 NRSV.

sermons, women maintained some distance between embodied preacherly life and embodied pregnant life. Such a space may have been precisely what they needed in order to preach.

While they did not share their pregnancy experiences within their sermons, these women did make rich theological connections between pregnancy and God. They spoke with passionate eloquence about the insights gained during pregnancy and childbirth. "My emotional understanding of the incarnation is much more personal now," said Rev. Harris. "Even now, baptism is so emotional. It is hard to get through the liturgy without choking up. In the fullness of time Jesus was nurtured in the water of a womb." Rabbi Levin reflected, "Pregnancy didn't change my theology as much as it affirmed it and strengthened it. A life being brought into this world—how can you not believe in God after that moment? I truly believe we have a partnership with God and that we're all created in the image of God." Such insights eventually wove their way into their sermons. But that happened later, after the baby was born. They chose to keep those connections to themselves while they were pregnant. When asked whether they brought illustrations of their pregnancies into the pulpit, women often responded with memories of sharing stories about raising children. As long as their bodies proclaimed the baby they refrained from mentioning it. In this way, the sermon functioned as another boundary.

Pregnant Identity: Intersections of Body and Self

Pregnancy caused women to be decentered, existing in a doubled space between their pre-pregnant and pregnant embodiments, between the needs of their growing babies and the calls of their congregations. Through Young's rich contributions, pregnancy can be understood as the process in which the boundaries do become fluid, as well as filled with possibility. To discover the expectant space as a place of fullness is the hope of every mother and quite possibly the hope of the God who was made flesh and dwelt in a mother's womb.

When caught up in the fluidity of pregnancy, these female preachers became especially attuned to the fluidity at work between themselves and their babies, between themselves and their congregations. As one set of boundaries broke down in their embodied lives, they created better boundaries in another arena. These decisions were intentional, self-conscious actions, but they flowed from immediate, lived experiences. "I realized I wasn't as public a person as I thought I was" and "I didn't know my limits until they exerted themselves" were apt phrases for the processes at work. One motivating factor for such boundary-making moments surely emerged from sensing their bodies were not their own. "My body is mine, but it is not mine" was a pregnant realization. Rev. Williams shared, "I kept saying to my husband, my body is no longer my own. Even my body isn't something I can lay claim to at this point." The assertion of stronger, more definite boundaries, created through limitations on what questions they would answer, what stories they would share, and who could touch their swelling bellies, came in response to a diminished sense of embodied ownership.

All of this body-talk pushed women into reflections about the self. Young argues that the doubling that occurs with pregnancy illustrates the falsity of a unified self. The self, she asserts, is a project, always in the process of enactment, and often enacted through contradiction. Pregnant preachers experienced that contradiction in concrete, recurring ways as they held together dual identities as preachers and potential mothers. Preaching while miscarrying, they knew in their materiality the contradictions of birth and death. Trying to preach with less than ample breath and a smaller bladder, they felt the tension of a body beyond their control and a sermon they were expected to preach. They also experienced the development of the self, as they found themselves speaking up when they previously might have been silent, being surprised by their boldness in setting limits, and gaining new nuances to long-held theological beliefs. The self was a self in process, a project always under construction. In both the tension of contradiction and the energy of growth, women expanded the boundary of the self.

Pregnancy further brought the conceptions of self and body together with greater urgency. Although an embodied self remains the most accurate terminology, intense physical changes created, at times, the illusion of a separation between mind and body, spiritual identity and the physical state. When trying to share these experiences women's language broke down. Terms like self and body seemed inadequate to fully delineate the events under discussion. They spoke in contradictions: my body but not my body, my changing self but the essence of me has not changed. A woman's efforts to set boundaries can be understood as a reassertion of the self during immense changes in the body. Can the self still be the self, when the body changes so much?

Rev. Williams delved most deeply into this topic. Having asserted that the body was only one aspect of one's overall identity, she returned to the topic in her post-pregnancy interview. Here, she wondered about the self and the body.

> For me it [pregnancy] made me realize that we are much more than our bodies. I was still the same person. You are changing and your identity is growing as you come to terms with being a new mom but the fundamental core of who I was hadn't changed any. And yet my body was so different than what it was. If my body was my identity and it stopped there, and then that sense of truly who I was would have changed a lot more in that process.

When asked to elaborate on what about the self had remained unchanged, Rev. Williams replied,

> I still knew myself to be a child of God. I still knew myself as one who laughs at all the same things and still finds the same things unnerving and still finds some things just unacceptable. All of the things that sort of end up creating this sense of identity hadn't really changed. It was just my body that was going through this really crazy time and so I don't really know how to name that.

A strict embodied approach might challenge Rev. Williams's words, asserting that the body's changes would inevitably change the self. It might be that Rev. Williams's insistence on not changing was a defensive stance. She asserted everything was the same just as everything churned in upheaval. But her openness to examine her pregnancy belies that idea. Another explanation might attribute her position to the long cultural history of placing women in close proximity to their bodies. Acquainted with the notion that a woman, especially a pregnant woman, was just her body, Rev. Williams adds to the equation other, important elements of her identity: her theology, her sense of humor, and her values. She drew a new line creating a continuum between her pre-pregnant and post-pregnant selves.

The notion of embodiment asserts that knowledge comes through our bodies. As Merleau-Ponty states, "Consciousness is always and everywhere incarnate." Every aspect of Rev. Williams's identity—the ongoing project of her self—is gained through bodily life. It stands to reason, then, that the self both shifts and stays continuous through pregnancy. Her embodied self reacted to pregnancy just as it had reacted to other major life events, such as adolescence, ordination, or marriage. Since pregnancy involves sharing physical space with another life, it can provide an awareness of the physicality of all life. The self is added to or enhanced, but doesn't lose touch with the self previously constructed. "I still knew myself to be the same person.

It was just that my body was changing so much" is an accurate depiction of the pregnant self.

Before, during, and after pregnancy, these women preached. The insights they discovered as pregnant preachers proclaim something about preaching. In the previous chapter's discussion of performance in preaching, Ward's assertion that a performance perspective deepens our understanding of "why we preach at all" was used to argue for an embodied understanding of proclamation. Ward emphasizes the preacher's embodied awareness of the other. He quotes Wallace Bacon, who states, "You cannot know yourself by yourself. You are you because you are not the other, but you can find yourself only by going out from yourself."[15] Ward concludes, "A performance-centered approach to preaching emphasizes that the aim of the preacher is to develop this sense of the other in the process and practice of preaching."[16]

Pregnancy is a profound time of othering. Rather than going outside the self to learn of the other, women looked inside to discover an "other" profoundly connected to them and also in the process of becoming not them. They came to know themselves by hosting the life of another. Such knowledge can and should enlarge our preaching. The pregnant preacher becomes reverently aware of "the opportunity to give voice and embodied presence to the other."[17] Rev. Williams's term for such othering was stewardship. She framed pregnancy as a process that deepened her understanding of being a steward of the world. Naming the holy discomfort of sharing the space of her body, she came to express her feeling of her body no longer being her own as an exercise in stewardship. Her grasp of embodied stewardship challenges preachers to think of their embodied proclamations within the same stewardship framework. Because she says it so well, she will have the last word.

> It really changed my understanding of the Holy Spirit. We always talk about the Holy Spirit being God in us and in other people, and to have this new life being birthed from within me made that more tangible for me. Sam has been his own person from the moment that he was conceived. [But] that something could be inside of me and a part of me and not me that really helped me understand the Holy Spirit better. I found myself often singing the song

15. Bacon, "Sense of Being," 139.
16. Ward, "Performance Turns in Homiletics," para. 38.
17. Ibid.

Sanctuary—Lord, make me a sanctuary—in that whole process.
Yeah, it was cool. And I'm not a singer.

Stewardship in preaching begins with the preacher's embodied existence. In Rev. Williams's experience, the challenges presented by pregnancy provided the possibility of deeper embodied knowledge. The potential for other ruptures within embodiment—and the women's movements in response—will be the focus of the next chapter.

.

CHAPTER 7

The Embodied Preacher: Appearances and Dys-Appearances

In the summer following third grade, the Reverend Jane Lee contracted polio after a swim in Lake Ontario. She spent weeks in the hospital, isolated from her family and from the freedoms of her childhood. She sensed—rather than saw—when a child down the ward died. Although she counted herself one of the lucky ones, sent home with working legs after the worst of the symptoms subsided, she would endure innumerable surgeries, countless weeks on crutches, and limited physical stamina for the rest of her life. "All of it became part of my identity," she said. Despite the challenges, she continued, "I was determined to be as normal as possible." So for decades she plowed through surgical reconstructions, returned to work in a walking cast, and learned to "push through the pain" when her body's cries were at odds with the demands of her life. She could do this, she said, "because the body is awesomely made. In polio the muscle fibers that were orphaned from the death of the nerve cells are innervated by adjacent muscles, who grow extra nerves, attach themselves to the orphaned fibers, and they began to work."

Several decades after the onset of the disease, polio survivors typically lose their remarkable capabilities. The muscles that grew extra nerves are now giant motor neurons. After years of supporting five hundred or more additional fibers, they experience metabolic fatigue. "They began to drop out," explained Rev. Lee, "and because they had taken over so many nerves, you would lose a lot of function quickly." Once able to sustain her identity as an "essentially able-bodied person with a little problem," she encountered the life-changing limitations of post-polio.

Ordained ministry was a second career for Rev. Lee, begun after a distinguished career as a librarian. When she had raced up and down the stairs of a multistoried library or sat down with children for story time, the postpolio symptoms of pain, fatigue, and limited mobility had been minimally present. Now they were on far greater display. She found herself sitting in the hospital lobby before visiting a parishioner, exhausted from the walk from her car to the building. A pastoral emergency or an overnight confirmation trip could leave her limping for days. And on the Sunday afternoons after she preached, she crawled into bed and slept until dinner.

Rev. Lee approached preaching with trepidation. She loved Scripture. She possessed the gifts of wise interpretation and precise, convicting words. She was a gifted storyteller. But she hated preaching. Serving as an associate minister, she did not preach weekly. But as preaching day loomed, her anxiety soared. She knew she could craft a good sermon on paper. She doubted her ability to deliver it. Specifically, she dreaded the physical hurdles she would face in attempting to perform it well. "First of all," she explained, "preaching is hard physically. It is. It is exhausting." Rev. Lee had dealt with occasional exhaustion at other points in her life. On rare occasions, she had had to rest for a couple of days after a busy work or family season. Preaching one Sunday's worth of sermons drained her completely. "I physically couldn't stand up for more than twelve to fifteen minutes," she said. "I always needed the lectern to hold on to, so I used only one-handed gestures and would pour energy into the intonations of my voice. And when the style of preaching moved to the more informal style, I couldn't do it." Her trepidation began before she reached the pulpit. "I always had anxiety about the steps [up to the pulpit]," she said. Whenever she climbed them "the awkwardness of my gait was embarrassing to me. It was very anxiety-producing, just the physical piece of getting up there and getting down." Thinking about her body throughout a sermon, preaching produced a sense of inability, as "I can't do that" became attached to its basic tasks. "My disability has informed my ministry in very significant ways," she concluded, "not just emotionally and spiritually but also the physical experience of it."

Rev. Lee was one of two preachers in this study whose preaching embodiments were informed by chronic physical conditions. The tasks associated with preaching—walking to the pulpit or stage, standing for a prolonged period, and using gestures—were more demanding for the individual whose body had less mobility, strength, or stamina. One might approach an exploration of Rev. Lee's preaching embodiments through the lens of disability. Post-polio syndrome would meet most understandings of what counts as a disability, generally defined as an impairment or restriction in a person's ability to perform a function to a typical standard evidenced across individuals or groups. Rev. Lee made use of some items that often count as markers of disability, including a handicap parking permit and, on occasion, a cane. And she sometimes described herself as disabled. When comparing her preaching to her colleagues, she judged herself as lacking the expected skills necessary for informal preaching or standing without a supportive hand on the pulpit. A framework of disability could help illumine some of these choices and experiences, and the ways they matter—and do not matter—to Rev. Lee and to her congregation.

While a disability framework can do important work, a lived body approach can do more to grasp how, using Merleau-Ponty's terminology, Rev. Lee's body "rises to her tasks." A lived body approach is less concerned with what Rev. Lee can or cannot do, because every body can and cannot perform some tasks, and more intrigued by how Rev. Lee lived in, with, and through the limitations and potentials of her body. A lived body approach shines a spotlight on how Rev. Lee experienced her body, wanting to examine when she was most cognizant of being bodily, when she made intentional uses of her body, and when her body's presence faded from conscious view. Every preacher had moments when her body's presence came to the forefront of her awareness, as well as moments when she forgot her body while preaching. Examining these rhythms of bodily presence and absence can deepen our understanding of the diverse approaches to embodied preaching.

The Absent Body: The Contributions of Drew Leder

In his phenomenological exploration of the body, Drew Leder poses "the question of why the body, as a ground of experience, tends to recede from direct experience."[1] While affirming Merleau-Ponty's orientation to the body as the mode and medium through which we experience the world, he argues that our primary experience of the body is often of its absence. Even though "human experience is incarnated" and "the body plays a formative role," Leder writes, "this bodily presence is of a highly paradoxical nature. While in one sense the body is the most abiding and inescapable presence

1. Leder, *Absent Body*, 1.

in our lives, it is also essentially characterized by absence."[2] Hoping to heal the long-standing opposition between mind and body, the abiding Cartesian paradigm, Leder illuminates how biological and physiological realities make the body disappear so long as it is functioning properly, only to reappear in prominent and problematic ways when dysfunction occurs.[3] "Certain modes of disappearance are essential to the body's functioning," he writes.[4] "These disappearances particularly characterize normal and healthy function."[5] Because we tend to think less about the body when it can fully "enact its projects" and find ourselves unable to stop thinking about the body when it breaks down or is in pain, the self becomes identified by cognition, the thinking we do when the body recedes, and the physical body, obvious in distress, is rendered an "it" opposed to us.[6] The disrupted body becomes separate from us, an "other" opposed to the self.[7]

A preacher who easily bounds up the pulpit steps and stands at will until she chooses to move may either forget her body, rendering it absent to her perception, or feel so alive to her movements that she feels free in her body, released from the prison of former constraints. Rev. Lee, awake to her pain and aware of her limits, will not forget her body. She might describe her body as absent, but here it was "the very absence of a desired or ordinary state."[8] She detailed her preaching through a series of tasks her body cannot do: I cannot preach beyond fifteen minutes, without holding on to the lectern, or in a relaxed, informal style. She experienced her body as constricting her preaching.[9] Leder terms this body the "dys-appearing" body. He writes, "In moments of breakdown, I experience to my body, not simply for it. In contrast to the 'disappearances' that characterize ordinary function, I will term this the principle of dys-appearance. That is, the body

2. Ibid.

3. In speaking of the body's processes, Leder writes, "The body falls back from its own conscious perception and control. As ecstatic/recessive being-in-the-world, the lived body is necessarily self-effacing" (ibid., 69).

4. Ibid.

5. Ibid.

6. Ibid., 76–77.

7. Ibid., 69–70.

8. Ibid., 4.

9. Speaking specifically about the impact of pain, Leder states, "The tendency of pain to disrupt our intentionalities never leads to a complete collapse of the world. However, the new world into which we are thrust by pain has a constricted aspect. We are no longer dispersed out there in the world, but suddenly congeal right here" (ibid., 75).

appears as thematic focus, but precisely as in a dys state."[10] Akin to persons with distress or disease engaged in other tasks, Rev. Lee's landscape for preaching is "viewed not as a field of possibility but of difficulties to negotiate. The ordinary sense of free and spontaneous movement is now replaced by calculated effort; one does not want to take chances."[11] In her most pain-filled or weakened state, the body "stands in the way, an obstinate force interfering with our projects."[12] Rev. Lee wanted to walk comfortably up to the pulpit. But her body slowed her down. She admired the easy stance of a colleague, who preached as if he were carrying on a conversation. But she must reckon with the exertion necessary for her to stand for fifteen minutes. Her body appeared precisely as a stubborn entity opposing her efforts to preach.

In seeking to explain why an embodied person can experience her physical body as such an oppositional or constraining presence, Leder uses a phenomenological lens to break apart the dualism of the body opposed to the mind. He argues that it is precisely our experiences of embodied living that encourage the body-mind split. The body becomes negatively associated with brute force because the cycle of absence in health and presence in breakdown encourage such conceptions.[13] Discussing the tenacious association of the self with the mind in Western thought, he asserts, "A phenomenological treatment of embodiment must not merely refute this view but account for its abiding power."[14] Drawing on the philosophical distinction between *Körper*, the physical body, and *Leib*, the living body, he suggests, "*Körper* is itself an aspect of *Leib*, one manner in which the lived body shows itself."[15] Thus, an individual's *Körper*, or physicality, is not reduced to mute or unthinking materiality but rather is an integral aspect enabling the *Leib*. Correspondingly, the *Leib*, encompassing the range of activities, cognitions, emotions, and intentionalities integral to embodied life, happens in, with, and through the body as an integrated whole.[16] Exploring the lived body as both *Körper* and *Leib* "reveals the deeper

10. Ibid., 83.
11. Ibid., 81.
12. Ibid., 84.
13. Ibid., 3–4.
14. Ibid., 69.
15. Ibid., 5.
16. Ibid., 6.

significance of corporeality as generative principle."[17] Leder acknowledges how one's experiential sense may remain "the recalcitrant body as separate from and opposed to the 'I,'" but he emphasizes that the sense of separation happens within the embodied self.[18] Even the sense that the body has separated from the mind occurs within an undivided embodiment. He explains, "As I look down on a paralyzed limb I may be struck by the alien nature of embodiment. But I still use my eyes in looking down, my nervous system in thought, my other limbs in compensation for the paralyzed one."[19] Embodiment becomes the fragile holding together of disparate pieces of living, which exhibit moments of powerful coalescence and which suffer moments of painful rupture. While Leder often uses the term body as a *Körper*, he searches for how the *Körper* shapes and is shaped by the *Leib*. That the *Körper* can be a generative force for the *Leib* creates new pathways toward healing the *Körper-Leib* divide and enabling every living body to find greater communion in the world.

Dys-appearance as a Mode of Analysis

It would be inaccurate to label the female body as an obstinate force to a woman's preaching. At the same time, many of the elements traced through Rev. Lee's narrative, including the recurring sense of the body as an "other" and the prevailing notion of preaching as a series of physical difficulties to negotiate, find translation in women's stories about their preaching bodies. In speaking of clothing and hairstyle choices, some women framed the body as a distraction that needed to be minimized. In recounting her efforts to improve her voice, Rabbi Levin named it a physical issue related to her ability to be heard and accepted as the preacher. In discussing her preaching gestures, Rev. Robinson confessed her impression of being wooden in the pulpit. Many women shared instances when others commented upon their physical appearance. While extreme, Rev. Lee's experience represents a commonly shared narrative of bodily dys-appearances among this group of female preachers. Gender, then, plays a role in how preaching bodies consistently dys-appear.

These preachers, though, did not report only moments of the body's appearance through dysfunction or nonconformity to accepted preaching

17. Ibid., 5.
18. Ibid., 88.
19. Ibid.

forms. They also shared instances in which the body receded from their awareness, becoming absent in its high-functioning state. The reoccurring reflection of talking with the hands was one attempt to put words to a well-performing body. Preaching with bare feet might be another. These experiences of the body's presence in absence, however, felt more complex and ambiguous than Leder's polarized dynamic of absence or dysfunction. An experience of talking with the hands or preaching without shoes resisted a single interpretation of embodiment. To understand how an individual preacher experienced her embodiment entails inquiries about how a preacher is alive in and to her body. She may explain her embodied choices as working *for* her body, and thus reveal herself as an embodied self. Alternatively, she might describe a preaching decision or movement as relating *to* her body, and thus demonstrate a split between the self as subject and her body as an object. Her sense of agency had a role in her understanding of and response to the ways her body dys-appears.

Leder's analysis of the body that recedes and reappears provides an avenue through which to study the female preacher's embodiments. In exploring the ways bodily absence and presence weave in and out of the lived experiences of these preachers, this chapter will also examine how preachers stretch toward self-conscious, purposeful embodiments within their preaching and how gender and agency influence those embodied events.

The Appearing and Dys-appearing Body during Preaching

Rev. Harris agreed that preaching is physical work. "Preaching is physically demanding for me, because I do use my whole body," she said. "But it is energizing too." She experienced times of being self-conscious about her body, especially the afternoon she officiated at a wedding while seven months pregnant. "I wore the wrong shoes and I was hot," she said. "My balance had changed and I couldn't stand in the heels. And I had worn a sweater underneath my robe. The whole time I was thinking how hot I was." Pregnancy is a time when the body reappears, made prominent by the physical shifts of housing a life and the socially sanctioned emphasis upon a pregnant woman's body. Rev. Harris experienced a different kind of embodiment on another Sunday, capping a sermon about how the Holy Spirit makes us move with a grand jeté down the aisle. "I was really anxious about it," she remembered. "Are people going to think this is weird? Am I going to be able to do it? But people's response was really good. And I thought, this is a totally different way of preaching."

Over the years of her preaching, Rev. Harris's body appeared and disappeared. Its appearance was emphatic, but not necessarily welcome or unwelcome. She could be uncomfortably aware of her physicality when unsteady and sweating. But she could also sense the energy, a whole new level of engagement for both her and the congregation when her body came to the forefront and performed well. At other times her body receded into the sermon but its absence was tempered by her sense of its creative strength. Her body mattered for preaching in many different ways, but it always mattered. She thought about its significance in theological language. Believing "we are made in the image of God" with "beautiful, amazing, and diverse bodies," she conceived of "the word of God dwell[ing] within us." She drew upon a Christian theory of the Word made flesh to conclude, "My role as the preacher is to give voice to that word of God, [so that] God wells up in other people." Using embodied life to inform her proclamation, she aimed toward nurturing a similar sacred embodiment in the listeners.

Other preachers also reflected the intermingling of body and theology as their preaching bodies were absent, present, and dys-appeared. Rev. Baker had a background in music, singing in various community choirs. Having described her preaching as a "whole body performance," she continued, "I use gestures, facial expressions, an intonation of voice, and my hands. When you are doing an opera, you are acting as well as thinking." Alongside words about using "everything I have to get the message across," she quickly added that once she is preaching, "I ignore my body." The body receded as it rises to its projects, performing in ways that fulfill and exceed its training. Rev. Baker valued this absence of her body from her consciousness. It is one reason she wears liturgical dress for worship. "The alb helps me ignore my body," she reported. "Once the robe goes on my body is a vehicle or a tool." The body reappeared, though, without its prescribed liturgical cover on the Sunday she inadvertently left her robe at home. "It was just a really strange feeling to be up there without it," she said. While she couldn't pinpoint the particular nature of her discomfort, she did assert, "I think women are looked at differently." Conscious of being looked *at*, she was distracted with thoughts about her clothing. She wondered if her sleeveless dress was appropriate for worship. Did it follow her form too closely? For a moment, she moved from living in her body to observing her body. The watchfulness reduced her body to a physical thing, which risked being seen and evaluated. In Leder's language, the absence of an alb made her body dys-appear.

A Social Dys-Appearance

Leder weaves through his analysis the reality that the embodied self is also inescapably social.[20] We recognize our embodied nature in communal spaces, "arising out of experiences of the corporeality of other people and of their gaze directed back upon [us]."[21] While one hopes the directed gaze affirms our situated life in the world, the gaze of others "can tear the body apart from itself," rendering a person highly conscious of her body as a *Körper*.[22] Leder identifies this as a "social dys-appearance," in which various groups of people are known only in and through their physicality. If "the primary stance of the Other is highly distanced, antagonistic, or objectifying" then the link of body to self—the link of *Körper* and *Leib*—is threatened.[23] Internalizing the objectified perspective of the Other, "I become conscious of myself as an alien thing. A radical split is introduced between the body I live out and my object-body, now defined and delimited by a foreign gaze."[24] Leder asserts that the power differential between genders has resulted in women being linked to their physicality. Attuned to the ways their bodies are observed and evaluated, women are more likely to devote energy to clothes, hairstyles, jewelry, and makeup. They contend with cultural representations that depict not diverse possibilities of embodiment but the female *Körper* as a strange, altered, or dangerous object.[25] In social dys-appearance, one does not experience her body as belonging to her. Severed from the self, the meaning of the body is interpreted by an external, powerful Other.[26]

During her years in ministry, Rabbi Levin learned how congregants watch her body. They have noticed, she said, "how my body has ebbed and flowed" through pregnancies, various hairstyles, and New Year's resolutions to join the gym. At the synagogue's gathering for Purim each year, she,

20. Ibid., 4–5, 34.
21. Ibid., 92.
22. Ibid., 96.
23. Ibid.
24. Ibid.
25. See Bordo, *Unbearable Weight*.
26. Leder, *Absent Body*, 98–99.

along with many children in the congregation, come in different costumes. One year, she wore a courtly ball gown, reminiscent of Queen Esther and similar in style to several younger girls. She recalled, "I looked so cute. I thought I looked like all the other little girls." The next year she wore a different costume. She continued, "Some of the dads were asking me if I was going to wear the same gown again. I realized that it was not so much that I was dressed like the little kids but the curvy nature of the dress." Such moments, she said, "are definitely times I'm very aware of my body." She continued, "There is a certain degree of neuteredness that comes with being a rabbi, but there are definitely times that they see me in a way that I'm clearly a woman." Rabbi Levin lived her rabbinical role closely attuned to her femaleness. She had her own experiences of childbirth. She had blessed newborn babies at hospitals. She felt keenly the miracle of "being with other people at that moment of birth or death." She conceived of her body as a sacred tool. She hoped her preaching brought listeners closer to the ways "our bodies are God's instruments to do God's will in the world." Intermingled with these powerful evocations was the vulnerability of being a woman. Even if it was a complimentary "you look great," Rabbi Levin never forgot "the fact that they are going to notice my haircut when I don't think they ever comment on a male rabbi's haircut or their shoes." When conscious that others were noting her physicality, she joined Rev. Baker in watching her body rather than living bodily. The hovering external gaze threatened her empowered embodiment while creating tension between corporeality and selfhood. With each body-directed compliment or criticism, she registered the risk of being owned by the congregation, always "amazed how much people saw [her] as their possession." Like many of the preachers in this study, Rabbi Levin oscillated between the moments when her body appeared, disappeared, and reappeared. When her body dys-appeared, the dys-appearance often could be attributed to the social dys-appearance of a female body. The gaze of the other was not all encompassing. Rabbi Levin retained her sense of embodied potential, naming the living body as a place of divine possibility. Yet the alternate possibility—to be owned by an outside earthly power—remained in her purview and created moments when the rift between physicality and self crept into her preaching.

Agency amid Absence and Dys-appearance

In his conceptions of the absent body and the dys-appearing body, Leder provides tools for grasping how embodied life comes in and out of view in the preaching experiences of these women. Of course, the preacher's body was always present. But the stories they shared illustrated the modes of absence, presence, and dys-appearance. A disability might prompt awareness of the body's presence, just as a flying leap down the aisle might awaken a preacher to her body's power. An unsolicited comment about her appearance might startle a woman into self-consciousness about her body. Leder's notion of social dys-appearance helps explain these phenomena. At the same time, the experience of dys-appearance never fully determined the actions women took. A preacher might cover her body with a liturgical robe. She might ask a stranger not to touch her pregnant belly. She might redirect a listener's provocative comment to her preaching or pastoral role. In the moments of dys-appearance, women made choices to repair the breach.

Furthermore, while Leder's structure of absence and dys-appearance emphasized the negative quality of the body's appearance to consciousness, these women also described how their body appeared in positive, empowering ways. "This is a totally different way of preaching," said Rev. Harris. Rev. Williams drew strength from her growing baby's movements as she wrote a sermon. Rev. Lewis felt energized on the Sunday she set her sermon to rap and danced alongside the youth who performed with her. Rabbi Kahn took pride in her strong, variable voice, saying, "It is a strength for me. I know when I stand in front of a group, I command attention immediately." Ms. Clark remembered intentionally raising and lowering her voice—playing with its power—when enacting a dialogue that began with a trembling Moses and a recalcitrant Pharaoh and turned into a confrontation between a defiant Moses and a frightened Pharaoh. She said, "The more relaxed I am, the more embodied I am. And the better I am with my body, the more I do feel present bodily, and I'm a better preacher when that happens." These preachers knew the power of their embodied lives.

Most notably, these preachers expressed a subtler blending of appearance, disappearance, and reappearance than Leder's opposing extremes. Even when it seemed the body completely receded, traces of embodiment were still experienced. Even when it appeared the body was a mere materiality, a brute obstacle to be overcome, the hopeful potency of one's living body came alive amid proclamation. Quite often preachers expressed that hopefulness in their conceptions of the body's role in preaching. Claiming the body as "a powerful tool," "an instrument for God's will," and a dwelling site for the word of God, these preacher demonstrated how maintaining an awareness of the *Körper* always involved in the *Leib* generated a deeper understanding of lived experience and of preaching.

Leder's theories can be enriched by careful attention to these experiences. In this study, one preacher stood out for the absence of her body within her reflections about her preaching. Her absent body was central to her experience and understanding of preaching. At the same time, an analysis of her preaching—and her words about preaching—revealed how a straightforward correlation between absence and presence does not fully represent the complexity of any living body.

The Absent but Present Preacher

Rev. Martin is the minister of a small, city congregation where she serves as the pastor, preacher, and music leader. Since "singing is [her] way of worshiping God," she enjoys being "fully engaged" with the praise team on Sunday morning until the sermon's beginning. When it is time to preach, she places her sermon outline on the pulpit and then "leaves it" to preach a message she hopes would "live" within the congregation gathered that day. Like many homileticians, she imagines preaching as a conversation between God, herself, and the congregation. As she tunes into God's presence during worship, she diverts her attention away from her body. When asked about her approach to preaching, she portrayed herself as unconscious of and unencumbered in her body's movements. "People say I preach with my whole body," she said. "Others will comment that I kick my legs, I use my hands, that my eyes preach. It is hard to hear talk about my facial expressions because I am not aware that I'm doing that. My body is generally the last thing I am thinking about."

Rev. Martin reiterated her lack of focus on her body frequently throughout her interview. She spent little time on bodily decisions prior to preaching. "As far as getting dressed for worship," she explained, "I'm pretty casual. It is no real effort. Something simple. A regular dress. I am limited in my makeup and small earrings." The de-emphasis on the body continued in the pulpit. She elaborated, "Preaching is God using me. For me, it is just not about my body. [While] I don't want people staring at me, I don't think preaching is about me. They don't need to remember what I looked

like." Amid these minimizations of the body, she also named her willingness to use her body. "When God is speaking you have to step outside your
comfort zone to do what God wants you to do. When it comes to God,
I'm uninhibited," she explained. "So God says leap, I leap. Run, run. Stand
still, stand still." Not thinking about her body, she employed her body in all
manners of movement. Using Leder's framework, her body was absent to
her awareness as it functioned well to her expectations.

Rev. Martin's conception of preaching was almost exclusively orien-
tated to God as the author, director, and ultimate end of her sermons. She
attributed her body's absence to her belief in God's transcendent, activating
presence. Through an entire sermon, she asks, "What do you want to say
to this, God?" Focused on divine movement rather than her body's movement, she nevertheless did move. She used her body to jump, kick, whisper,
wave, walk, and stand still. Daringly free in her body, Rev. Martin professed
no premeditated plans or post-sermon knowledge of these actions. She
even suggested a bodily disconnect amid the sermon. She said, "In preaching, sometimes I feel like and people will tell you, it is another person. They
know it is my voice. But even for me it is an out of body experience." This
out-of-body moment, of course, happened through embodiment. Open to
her body, her body became less and less present to her. Becoming less and
less conscious of her body, she used her body more and more.

Interspersed with her body-effacing words were layers of bodily
awareness. Rev. Martin thus far has avoided watching videotapes of her
sermons. Yet she voiced a longing to observe her preaching face, a tacit
acknowledgment of the rhetorical power of nonverbal expressions. She
professed a long-held disinterest in her body's presentation, saying "I was
never one of those girls who cared much about her appearance." But she
wore well-crafted, elegant clothes and straightened her hair to lie simply
around her shoulders. It may be that not caring about her appearance
equaled a well-chosen but pared-down self-presentation. And it may be
that she had nurtured habits of dress such that her choices did not require
much thought or planning. Her choices reflected some level of embodied
awareness, an awareness that her absent body did not erase entirely.

Embodied awareness also emerged in her stories about her relationship with her listeners. She described how she uses her body to strengthen
the connection between pulpit and pew. When she first began preaching,
Rev. Martin was a manuscript preacher. She felt a distance with the congregation, as if the papers formed a wall between preacher and listeners.

Subsequently her hope became "to be that person who knew her manuscript verbatim. I would love to have every word so polished." But even when she preached from a memorized manuscript, she said, "I was still thinking 'okay what word now.' I couldn't connect with the congregation." One Sunday, she inadvertently left her written sermon at home. Forced to preach without it, she realized "it felt like freedom." From that experience, she learned, "I can let go. I can trust God in this." She also gained a new reliance on her body's knowledge. Firm in the need for a sermon to live, she felt a sermon come to life when her eyes left the printed page and focused upon the listeners' reflecting gazes. "I had every 'i' dotted and every 't' crossed," she said, "but when I have your eye, I could reach you in some way beyond reading the manuscript or even memorizing it." Rev. Martin identified her efforts to be acutely alert to what is occurring within the worshiping congregation and to God's leading as the foundational knowledge for each sermon. She then conceived of acquiring that knowledge through her interactions with other people's bodies. "For some reason, I need to touch you," she reflected later. "I may not know what is going on but if I can hug you, touch you [then] I can tell how you are doing." Having described preaching as an out-of-body experience, Rev. Martin also used her material being—and the physicality of others—to increase her connections to her listeners. Although her body remained an absent body, working in expected and habituated ways that keep those bodily deployments from presenting themselves too strongly in her consciousness, Rev. Martin had not lost touch with her body's capacity for insight. Leder argues that the intellect grows out of basic sensory perception.[27] Correspondingly, Rev. Martin's groundedness in the embodied interactions between herself and her listeners increased her perception of the needs within a worship service. Living as a body profoundly present in its absence, she gleaned from her embodied knowledge skills to increase the power of her preaching.

Rev. Martin's preaching body illustrates precisely Leder's phenomena of a body that recedes from awareness as it performs within the world. Claiming, "Preaching is not about my body," she exemplified a living body engaged in preaching. "The body is 'absent' only because it is perpetually outside itself," writes Leder, "caught up in a multitude of involvements with other people, with nature, with a sacred domain."[28] Rev. Martin's body faded into the background as she moved deeper into involvement with God

27. Leder, *Absent Body*, 7.
28. Ibid., 4–5.

and the congregation. She experienced herself as outside of her body, not because she has become disembodied but because her conscious attention had become so fully engaged beyond herself. At the same time, Rev. Martin maintained a tacit awareness of her integral embodiment. Her *Körper* generated new manifestations of her—and her congregation's—*Leib*.

Although existing on the far side of embodied preaching descriptions, Rev. Martin was not the sole preacher to describe moments of bodily presence through absence. Rev. Anderson once had the refrain from "Blessed Assurance" resonate in her spirit all through the week. "By Sunday," she remembered, "it was so deep within." She asked the musician to play the chorus following the sermon. Feeling propelled to do so; she walked down into the congregation and began dancing. "I grabbed one [congregant] by the arm and swayed and then went to another and swung [them around]. It wasn't a conscious thing. It happened. Afterwards I felt, 'Gosh that was foolish. What are they going to say?' But I haven't heard anything back at all." When sharing the story, Rev. Anderson placed it alongside an earlier time in her preaching when the child of a friend, visiting from out of town, had commented after church, "Pastor Joan, why are you standing there so stiff? It is like you are scared." Acknowledging, "I think she was right," she presented her morning of dancing as a time she felt free of any constraint and able to be a body moving in surprising and risky ways.

What set apart the episodes narrated by Rev. Anderson and Rev. Martin—as well as Rev. Harris's grand jeté and Ms. Clark's dialogical sermon—was the absence of self-consciousness. While she would worry—"Do parishioners think I am a simple-acting pastor?"—after the service, *during* the service Rev. Anderson was engrossed in her body. The significance of these experiences did not lie in the specifics of the movements. Dancing is not more embodied than standing still. Instead, the instances were marked by the preacher's work to set aside or lift the constraints accompanying bodily dys-appearance. Not distracted by being watched as an object, the preachers experimented with liberating uses of their bodies. Each of these instances displayed how female preachers found ways to embody their sermons. Upon choosing such empowering embodiments, they were drawn to continue to be physically present, buoyed by their own experiences of a body present to a sermon and their congregation's presence to their preaching. The meaning of the sermon lived in and through the body. And in their bodies, women glimpsed transcendence.

The Too-Present Body

Alongside moments of transcendence were moments in which the concrete needs of a preacher's specific materiality necessitated time, attention, and purposeful care. Rev. Lee, whose story opened this chapter, presented an intense example of a body requiring additional support. Most preachers in this study possessed bodies that functioned reasonably well. These preachers dealt with what they experienced as more mundane challenges, like an unfamiliar accent, a rickety knee, or, as in the case of Rabbi Levin, a short stature. When Rabbi Levin preached, she needed a step stool to be seen from behind the pulpit. Even then, she said, "I'm still not always sure if the people in the back row can see my full face or just the top." As she dealt with the logistics of keeping the stool at the ready, she was continually alert to how her height caused her body to dys-appear and how to interpret her embodiment for the congregation.

Rabbi Levin typically put the step stool in position behind the pulpit prior to a worship service. Occasionally, the custodian would pass through the sanctuary and unknowingly return the stool to its storage place. When Rabbi Levin shared a service with another rabbi or a cantor, the stool needed to be moved whenever her colleague spoke. The movement of the stool—behind the pulpit, away from the pulpit, and then back again—created an additional tier of negotiations. "It is a challenge," she acknowledged. "Just figuring out the dynamics is an extra piece of the puzzle." The moment of ascending the stool becomes quite noticeable on those occasions when she had "to bend down and make a point of pulling it out." She added, "It doesn't pull out easily, especially if you are wearing heels."

The actions around the step stool directed her and others' attention to her height. That focus only increased in services that included youth. When she stepped onto the stool at a bar or bat mitzvah, she occasionally referred to herself as "the one who looks like a bat mitzvah kid." She joked about being "the rabbi who has to stand on the stool to meet you eye to eye" and she grew to expect a soft ripple of laughter whenever she had to set the stool into place. In fact, humor became one of the main avenues through which she acknowledged her height. During her interview she characterized her responses to her step stool maneuvers as the choice either "to laugh, ignore it, or to be self-deprecating." Although Rabbi Levin appreciated the light-heartedness of these moments, she also admitted her conflicted emotions. "I don't wish I were taller," she said, "[but] we're about something very serious and there is a moment of laughter first. It takes away from what I'm going to say." She categorized her height as "something that I struggle with in terms of my identity as a rabbi." In the pulpit and beyond, "there are settings in which people don't see [me]." Not sure if they actually fail to see her or fail to see her as the rabbi, she simply termed those moments as times when "I'm not as visible."

When the body does not rise to its tasks in the ways we desire, argues Leder, it appears as "thematic focus."[29] In these situations, the body—in its pain, disease, or limitation—becomes the locus of attention and mode for interpretation. Life revolves around the themes inherent in the unfolding dilemmas of the body. At other times, the challenges of an individual's physicality become prominent through a prompt from the person. Self-conscious of a body's quirk or minor challenge, a preacher might accentuate that aspect of physical existence, potentially extending its presence and influence. In these instances, "thematizing about the body can itself bring about dysfunction."[30] Like a piano player who suddenly can't play because he or she is too self-conscious about how the fingers are finding the keys, the preacher may become so engrossed in handling a troublesome trait of her physicality that she diminishes some of her embodied capacities.[31] Understandably vigilant about the stool's presence and placement, Rabbi Levin often relied upon humor at her own expense to ease the awkward transition. But her joking manner risked drawing more attention to her height. She sensed how laughter robbed the sermon's beginning of its solemnity and how perceptions around her height potentially decreased her visibility.

The temptation to purposefully frame the conversation around her body was present for any preacher concerned with how the idiosyncrasies of her body appeared to the congregation. Whether it was the disability of polio, the weeks of a pregnancy, a temporary shift to street clothes rather than a robe, or an unusual height, a preacher might feel inclined toward interpreting her body solely through that mode of embodiment. She might become excessively explanatory or overly dismissive of her bodily differences in ways that increase the listeners' attention. She might make jokes about her body. Each mode of response, though, risked overwhelming her

29. Ibid., 83.

30. Ibid., 85.

31. Leder writes, "Self-awareness can allow us to seek help and effect repair. However, it can also exacerbate problems, intensifying anxiety or a slump in performance" (ibid., 85).

preaching by making her and others acutely consciousness of her body's presence. The desire to publicly promote a specific understanding of her body may be strengthened by the preacher's femaleness. With social dys-appearance placing an emphasis on her physicality, the female preacher becomes habituated to being hyper-conscious about every sound, step, or shift of her body. She may well stumble in her body just as the pianist tripped on her newly remembered fingers. The preacher who thematized her body risked splintering the body from the self. Rabbi Levin knew her innate pulpit skills. She remembered the congregant who emailed her to say, "I loved your sermon. You are a born rabbi." But her light-hearted call and response with the congregation offered a regular, poignant reminder of her bounded embodiment. At its best, thematized embodiment can generate critical reflection that leads to a renewal in preaching. At its worst, it can deepen the rift between body and self.

Every preacher preaches with and through bounded embodiment. And in those embodiments, every preacher makes choices about how to conceive of, explain, or promote the facts of her physicality. Rabbi Levin weighed her choices around acknowledging her height, knowing that it would be noticed whether or not she mentioned it. She then exercised her agency by choosing humor. The implications of her choice were readily apparent in her ambivalence, her wondering if humor decreased her rabbinical role. Simultaneously, the stool functioned as an important symbol in her preaching. She needed it in order to preach. More importantly, to dismiss the stool was to dismiss the particularities of her body. Without a connection to the specificity of her body a preacher risks losing the power of her own embodiment. There is no easy, perfect, or permanent answer to avoiding the instances in which the body stumbles over itself to become thematized to consciousness. The choosing, acting preacher continually moves between acknowledging how the body dys-appears and recasting those dys-appearances into vital ways in which the body connects to, informs, and is the self.

Standing Up to Preach

Each of the women in this chapter addressed the ways the body comes in and out of focus during preaching. The moments of appearance, disappearance, and dys-appearance shaped their experience of preaching and the meaning they attached to their preaching. The choices they made when the body came more prominently into view enabled subsequent embodiments. Since every embodiment had accompanying strengths and limitations, the critical task for each preacher arose in how she found ways to maintain and strengthen the connections between her physicality, selfhood, and proclamation. One preacher living with a congenital disease synthesized the paradoxical pieces of body and preaching in such a way that embodied life fed into embodied preaching. A close listening to her narrative reveals how the rhythms of embodiment—its connections and ruptures, its presence and absence—informed her understanding of herself as preacher and her preaching.

Ms. Clark was born with a mild case of cerebral palsy. This disease of the central nervous system is "characterized by paralysis, weakness, incoordination, or any other aberration of motor function."[32] Having worn leg braces as a child, Ms. Clark now walks with a barely noticeable limp. She has diminished mobility and near normal strength, as well as a sense of humor and a self-professed love of talking. When asked to talk about her disease, she presented an upbeat, almost casual attitude. "I've never thought about it," she replied. "Sometimes I limp and sometimes I do not. As I age, the limp can be there more often. It hasn't affected my actual life very much." She characterized her occasional limps as a small inconvenience among a larger sense of health. Maintaining the same tone when the topic changed, Ms. Clark downplayed the effects of cerebral palsy on her preaching performance. She acknowledged, "My balance under stress can be worse than my balance normally and the stage we preach on wobbles a bit." She categorized a single instance when she gripped the music stand throughout a sermon as a distraction quickly resolved by the next Sunday. "I'm not particularly excited to do a lot of walking around," she continued. "I pretty much stay in one place. I don't know how much of it is cerebral palsy and how much of it is new preacher who doesn't want to be away from her notes." While her cerebral palsy played a prominent role in her responses to questions about bodies and preaching, Ms. Clark consistently minimized its significance. Like Rev. Lee's early determination to "be as normal as possible," Ms. Clark appeared to be working to decrease its impact on her experiences of her body's presence. Yet, her body did dys-appear through her limps, unsteady balance, and occasional fatigue. She seemed caught between a dys-appearing body and her hopes for an absent one.

32. Cruickshank, *Cerebral Palsy*, 1.

The paradox of dys-appearance and absence continued when Ms. Clark answered a question about her theology of the body. She first replied, "I don't think I am as into my body as other people are. I don't care about my hair or my makeup. I have always been that way about my body. I think it is rooted in the CP." In this response, Ms. Clark used her disease to diminish the other manners in which the body can appear, stating that she simply didn't think about the adornments connected to her bodily presence. Leder named how the dys-appearing body possessed an absence characterized by the "absence of a desired or ordinary state."[33] Ms. Clark separated out her thoughts about her body from her perceptions of others' thoughts about their bodies. This may indicate her lack of concern for other types of body appearances and disappearances. It may also hint to a fissure between her body and her self, her *Körper* and her *Leib*.

After a brief silence, Ms. Clark offered more. "I think incarnation. God came in a body, that God suffered in a body is valuable to me. You walk this line between saying, 'Your body is not all of who you are' and saying, 'Look, claim your body.' To someone with a birth issue, you can say, 'You are beautifully and wonderfully made.'" With her second response, Ms. Clark introduced two views of the body that appear slightly contradictory at first glance. Understanding the body as mere physicality might lead a person to profess, "Your body is not all of who you are." Affirming the need to "claim your body" moved closer to embracing the *Körper* as one aspect of the *Leib*. As Ms. Clark traveled the boundary between materiality and lived body, she named the rupture in a way that offered avenues for healing it. Between "your body is not all of your identity" and "claim your body, wonderfully and beautifully made" there was room for growth, not away from the body but within the body's knowledge. Merleau-Ponty wrote, "We have found underneath the objective and detached knowledge of the body that other knowledge which we have of it in virtue of its always being with us and of the fact that we are our body."[34] It is this embodied knowledge carried within our living existence that Ms. Clark pointed toward in the paradox of physical body and living self.

Ms. Clark loves to preach. She called preaching "the most important thing I do, the most life-giving thing, the thing that if they took everything else away and let me have it, it would be enough." Although initially presenting an attitude toward embodiment that minimized both her disease

33. Leder, *Absent Body*, 4.
34. Merleau-Ponty, *Phenomenology of Perception*, 239.

and her body, Ms. Clark grew more realistic about her living body's barriers as she spoke about the way she felt her body's presence when she preached. Preaching became the moment when she encircled her *Körper* into her *Leib*. Ms. Clark said, "I think having cerebral palsy is why I put so much weight on the moment of rising to your feet in that moment after the anthem or whatever comes before preaching. There is the silence and the waiting and I feel the congregation waiting and the act of standing is my moment of decision as a preacher." Every time she stood, amid the "O God, here we go sort of feeling" in the pit of her stomach, she was conscious "that the instant where your brain sends the impulse to your leg muscle is my moment of faith confession. It is a courageous and crazy act of faith to stand up to go to the pulpit." The biology behind rising to her feet was not lost on Ms. Clark. "I think," she said, "cerebral palsy makes that moment what it is for me, because it is more work for me to stand and remain standing in a very subtle way than [for] most and so I ground my preaching there." The dys-appearance of her body became a resource for her testimony.

A preacher's experiences of the body's dys-appearance, then, are not solely negative or constricting experiences. When the body appeared by virtue of an injury, disease, or lack of ability, an individual gains valuable knowledge about how her living body was grounded in materiality. She learns the resource of her living body. New avenues are forged into the knowledge within the body, a symbol of the generativity inherent at all levels of lived existence. And with new knowledge, a person discovers new methods for agency. Interestingly, Ms. Clark's body did not recede from her consciousness when she stood. Instead, she was able to stand precisely out of an intimate, embodied knowledge of the cost of her standing. With that, she learned anew the power of her ability to move. Characterizing the moment as her confession of faith, Ms. Clark accessed the awesome wonder with which the body is made, the possibilities on her own embodied agency—her choice to stand and confess—and the sacred link between her living body and God's speech.

The Embodied Preacher: Appearances and Dys-appearances

Like Ms. Clark's ability to glean knowledge from her body's dys-appearance, the intermingling of appearance, disappearance, and dys-appearance across these female preachers witnessed to the power of bringing the body into one's consciousness. In many respects, the guiding goal of this study has been to illumine the body's appearance within the self-reflective, purposeful choices of these preachers. Even those moments when the body first is present as an obstacle could be occasions for deeper knowledge, greater agential power, and more faithful proclamation. Whether it was Rev. Martin's commitment to leap when God says leap, Rabbi Levin's deliberations about how to interpret her shorter statute, Rev. Baker's willingness to use voice and hands, or even Rev. Lee's trepidation to listen to her body's pain, every time a woman worked to integrate her materiality into her lived body, she increased her ability to act as a body. To act as a body did not mean that every preacher strove toward Rev. Martin's absent yet present body. Nor did it mean that escaping the effects of post-polio was the only avenue for greater embodiment available to Rev Lee. Rather, these preachers acted as a body as they deepened their awareness of the body's knowledge, the wisdom we possess by virtue of "the fact that we are our body."[35] Since agency rested in the body, the capacity for choice increased as the women grew more and more present to their embodied existence.

Alongside considerations of agency, Leder's theory of social dys-appearance raised questions about the role gender plays in these preachers' embodiments. Leder argued that the female body dys-appeared as women took in the objectifying gaze of society and were culturally conditioned to pay close attention to their bodies. The women in this study experienced that kind of gendered dys-appearance. They described constant, close attention to and consciousness of the body. The dys-appearing body contributed mightily to their experiences of preaching. Rabbi Levin's sense of her congregation's ever-watchful eye upon her body stood as a stark reminder about how the impact of a body even partially split from the self can diminish embodied life.

Yet the women in this study also lived and preached beyond such ruptures. They used such dys-appearances to generate new testimonies about embodied life. Grappling with how and why the body presented as an obstacle, they moved more deeply into their flesh and gained greater appreciated for the sacred meanings held within bodily life.

Reflections on her cerebral palsy led Ms. Clark into talk of incarnation. Preaching through a miscarriage strengthened Rev. Lockhart to affirm the resurrection. Setting boundaries around her pregnant body allowed Rev. Williams to form more authentic connections with her congregation. Speaking specifically about the biology of the body, Leder argued that every

35. Merleau-Ponty, *Phenomenology of Perception*, 239.

person is "sustained through a deeper 'blood' relation with the world."[36]
With bones bearing the same calcification as the inanimate world and cells
playing host to millions of bacteria, "my body everywhere bears the imprint
of Otherness."[37] Learning of otherness may well be the gift of a body's dys-
appearances. Corresponding to the ways a performance in preaching can
reach out to the other of text or audience and to the ways pregnancy can enlarge an individual's capacity for that which is other to us, a dys-appearing
body can serve as an occasion for a preacher's recognition of the otherness
contained in her flesh. Such recognition itself is a form of embodiment, an
othering that assists a woman who wants to embrace her own preaching
body, and, as that body, reach out to others and to God.

36. Leder, *Absent Body*, 66.
37. Ibid.

CONCLUSION

Embodied Preaching, Embodied Faith

A preacher's bodily life is inescapably involved with her preaching. We are our bodies when we preach. What began as a study of the discrete decisions a preacher made about her clothes, accessories, hairstyle, preaching position, voice, and gestures developed into an exploration of her embodiment. Embodiment encircles the physical body and the living self, for how we live cannot be separated from the form by which we live. Embodiment goes beyond materiality, acknowledging, as Merleau-Ponty asserts, that we are a "being in the world" and thus endlessly intertwined within a wider community that transmits a culture, religious tradition, messages about gender, and the practices of a specific worshiping community. To speak of embodiment is to reach for the collection of habitations and movements one acquires on the journey toward a competent, meaning-making self.

Too often conversations about embodiment, while soaring in their eloquence, veer away from the actual body. Fleshly life is messy, full of complex and competing choices, with both potential and peril, with meanings that are easy to discern, hypothesized perceptions that miss the mark, and mysteries to endlessly ponder. The impetus for this research originated in the female preacher who wondered why her body garnished so much attention, both her own attention in discerning how to present herself and the attention of her congregation who freely and frequently commented on her body. A preacher can hear that her body is vital to her sermon and be perplexed by the kind of focus her body receives. She can believe her body is integral to her preaching performance and feel frustrated when such awareness deters rather than encourages her embodiment. Leder's articulation of a dys-appearing body provides insight into the social forces that can promote looking at the body rather than living as a body. Women who speak in public arenas do so carrying the historical weight of past eras, which judged her body out of place. One connecting theme within this study traces the series of dys-appearances women encountered while preparing to preach and preaching.

This narrative thread often surfaced when women articulated their dilemmas around distraction. From a congregant who commented about her hair to the hesitation about formfitting clothes, women experienced their bodies as having the potential to distract. Distractability was a consideration in several embodied decisions and existed as an ever-present concern. Most often, the source of the distraction originated in their femaleness. Clothes that clung to the body might reveal the chest. Friday night's shoes worn on Sunday morning might raise eyebrows about the preacher's sexual status. A higher, softer voice risked comparison to a lower-pitched, more forceful one. In these moments a woman experienced her body as a hurdle to be overcome. The impediments registered at a deeper level, spilling beyond shoes, hair, or voice into a generalized questioning about one's ability to fulfill the task. In these moments, her embodiment risked being a hindrance to her preaching rather than a source of strength.

Existing alongside this narrative was a story about agency. As the spark that ignited an action, each woman made a choice as she considered how to best embody her preaching. Agency is often conceived as a straightforward dichotomy between freedom and constraint, even as theorists argue for a more nuanced understanding. When beginning this research I assumed a plotline would emerge detailing how female preachers threw off pulpit restrictions and wrestled out bodily freedom. In reality, agency is a far more complicated thread to untangle. What looked like a choice toward freedom—a rebellious decision to keep fingernails painted a bold color or to preach with enhanced theatrics—proved to be a choice also shaped by culture. Every choice illuminated now deeply bound a preacher was to her history, her body, her tradition, and her context. Such insights are not necessarily negative ones. Merleau-Ponty argues we can only choose because we have a field within which to choose. Miraculously, by existing in that field we become free. The limits of human agency can uncover the infinite power of God at work in each preacher's fleshly life.

A third, most compelling narrative appeared around the body's role as a tool or a vessel for preaching. Women recognized that to proclaim was to embody. Drawing from the wellspring of embodied life, they discovered ways for the insights, habits, and moves of their bodies to serve their preaching. They danced, jumped, and acclimated to their particular voices. One climbed a ladder. Another used intentional theater. A few made bodily choices and simply stated, "This is me." Many put on the attire that signified their faith, ushering themselves into sacred space. Several drew a boundary around their pregnant selves and discovered greater confidence in their preaching. One stood up to preach, grounding her proclamation in her body's willingness to rise. Their stories demonstrated how meaning is made through a living body's inter-involvement in her world. Their preaching embodiments also testified to the ways the human body, in which we "live and move and having our being" is a means by which God is revealed in the world.[1] As Luke Timothy Johnson writes, "The privileged arena for divine disclosure is the human body."[2]

For understandable and obvious reasons, homiletical conversations have privileged language in discussions about preaching, even while affirming the importance of the preacher's embodied, performing presence. But whether the goal of preaching is to mediate an encounter between God and humankind or to continue the conversation between listener, preacher, and God, our grasp of what happens when we preach and our vision for the aim of every sermon is enhanced by a belief in the body's capacity to confess God's presence and activity in the world. Johnson argues that our ordinary embodiments serve as the medium through which God is revealed.[3] Thus, exploring a preacher's bodily choices and behaviors is not undertaken simply to analyze the interworkings of physicality, culture, and choice but to marvel at the ways such inter-involvements can enable transcendence. Transcendence happens when a preacher makes space beyond her bound self for another self, in all the other's needs, longings, and giftedness, and makes space for God's spirit to appear.[4] These preachers spoke of such revelatory power. "If we are created in the image of God, then our bodies are part of how we get closer to God," said Rabbi Levin. "The eyes

1. Acts 17:28 NRSV.

2. Johnson, *Revelatory Body*, ix.

3. Ibid., viii.

4. Johnson defines transcendence as a "going beyond" that enables what is inside or interior to one body to become inside and interior to another. He writes, "Such human experiences of embodied spirit encourage us to imagine, in turn, with Scripture, God as spirit. As in the case of human transcendence, we imagine God's spirit also as involving embodiment" (ibid., 76).

are the window to the soul, that is true. They are windows to God as well. I see my body as a vessel, God's instrument to do God's will in the world," she continued. "Preaching," said Rev. Martin, "is about God using me." Rev. Harris spoke, in Christian terms, of embodying the Word. "My role as the preacher," she said, "is to give voice to God's Word so that God wells up in other people."

This view of the body's role in preaching is not new. The Apostle Paul conceived of his evangelical vocation, and the suffering he endured while preaching Christ crucified, as manifesting in his bodily life.[5] He named the thorn in his flesh and the marks branded on his body as signs of how Christ's power took root in him.[6] In 2 Corinthians 4, Paul reminded the early church that an earthly, breakable vessel can carry God's infinite, undefeated life, like a treasure held in clay jars. Upon enumerating the obstacles that have challenged but not defeated them, he concluded, "We carry in the body the death of Jesus, so that the life of Jesus may also be made visible in our bodies."[7] Here Paul was describing what he had learned and was still learning. By proclaiming the good news of God's salvation, Paul experienced Jesus's death dwelling intimately within him. Mysteriously, his lived experience of holding death made space for Christ's resurrected life. Paul located this sacred dynamic as happening in his body, an embodied reversal by way of his past, present, and future proclamation.

"When we preach," reflected Rev. Harris, "we are exposed, we are vulnerable, and we are doing something profound." We preach with imperfect, limited bodies, open to another's judgment or even suspicion. And yet in offering our bodily lives as spaces through which God can be revealed, we enter into a sacred process beyond ourselves, a dynamic that can turn injury into wisdom, suspicion into strength, limitation into liberation, death into life. By taking in his body the convictions that he preached, Paul learned of another knowledge; that God's transforming, divine power also was lodged in his body. This truth is available for every preacher. Through our embodied lives, we learn how to proclaim. We learn something of the truth that exists beyond our speech. As we experience in our bodies that transforming space, the mysteriousness of the process reminds us we are merely vessels and instruments, called into service by God who is always at work and always working to shine through our preaching.

5. Brenneman, *Embodiment in Paul.*

6. 2 Cor 12:7–9; Gal 6:17 NRSV.

7. 2 Cor 4:10 NRSV.

APPENDIX A

Description of Research

This is a qualitative study, in which the researcher understood herself as a participant-learner and assumed an interpretive, naturalistic approach. Qualitative research begins from a critical, inductive stance. Using a set of standard questions as a guide, the researcher asked broad, open-ended questions in hopes of understanding the experiences of female preachers as they describe them. It is expected that the study and subsequent scholarship will be guided by the gathered research and will shift in focus as the interviews proceed.

This research project was designed to explore the ways female preachers present, use, and experience their bodies as they prepare to and are preaching. The aim of the research focused on delving more deeply and understanding more clearly the female preacher's experience of embodied life and how those experiences influenced their practices and understandings of preaching. The research was comprised of three parts: individual, one-on-one interviews, a small group interview, and observations of the women preaching. The questions contained in the interviews included inquires about how an individual prepares her body to preach, the factors affecting her decisions about clothing, hairstyles, jewelry, and makeup, the times when the individual experienced her body detracting or supporting her preaching and any experiences of preaching while pregnant, if applicable. The small group questions were developed from the responses in the one-on-one conversations. In this interview, the group of women were asked to reflect on language used around bodily attractiveness and bodily distraction, their understanding and connection to female preachers across history, and to discuss together the implications of different theologies of preaching on how they think about and present their bodies.

APPENDIX B

Question Guide for One-on-One Interviews

1. Preparing the Body to Preach
   - What is your typical routine for preparing to preach?
   - Describe how you typically prepare your body to preach. What do you wear, including makeup, shoes, and jewelry?
   - What factors affect your decisions about dress?
   - How do you style your hair when you preach? Why?
   - As you prepare your body to preach, do you aim for a certain persona or style? If so, what factors affect your chosen style?
   - Have you ever radically changed your physical appearance while you have been preaching regularly? If so, what factors led to the change? How did the congregation receive you?
   - As you think about your decisions in regards to clothes, hair, or jewelry, what factors weigh most heavily upon your decisions?

2. The Body Preaching
   - Describe your preaching voice, including the rate, range and volume you typically employ when you preach? How does the congregation receive your voice?
   - What gestures do you typically use as you preach?
   - Describe the physical space in which you preach. Do you feel comfortable in the physical space? Is it too small or too large for your physical frame?

- Have you ever felt constrained by your body as you preach? If so, describe.

- Have you ever felt empowered by your body as you preach? If so, describe.

- What comments or feedback have you received specifically relating to your body from your congregation?

- Describe your style of preaching.

- Do you ever—for the sake of preaching—wish your body were different than it is? If so, what kind of body do you find yourself wishing for? If not, why?

- What is the role of the body in preaching?

- What is your theology of preaching?

3. The Body in General

- What is your theology of the body?

- How do you feel about your body on most days?

- How do you think about your body's role in preaching?

4. Pregnancy

- Have you ever preached while pregnant? If so, describe your experience.

- How did you dress when you preached? How did you make decisions about attire?

- How did the bodily changes of pregnancy affect your preaching?

- What was your congregation's reaction to your pregnancy?

5. Preaching Models

- Who do you identify as your preaching models? What preachers do you really admire? What do you remember about their bodies? Their preaching styles?

- Tell me about the first time you heard a woman preach. What was she wearing? What did she look like? What did you notice about her?
- Tell me about a preacher who rubs you the wrong way. What don't you like about his or her preaching style, voice, or appearance?

Bibliography

Allen, Ronald J. *Preaching: An Essential Guide*. Nashville: Abington, 2002.

Austin, Gilbert. *Chironomia; or, A Treatise on Rhetorical Delivery*. Edited by Mary Margaret Robb and Lester Thonssen. Carbondale: Southern Illinois University Press, 1966.

Bacon, Wallace. "A Sense of Being: Interpretation and the Humanities." *Southern Speech Communication Journal* 41 (1976) 135–41.

Banks, Ingrid. *Hair Matters: Beauty, Power, and Black Women's Consciousness*. New York: New York University Press, 2000.

Barrett, Elisa Erikson. *What Was Lost: A Christian Journey through Miscarriage*. Louisville: Westminster John Knox, 2010.

Bartow, Charles L. "The Delivery of Sermons." In *The Concise Encyclopedia of Preaching*, edited by William H. Willimon and Richard Lischer, 100–101. Louisville: Westminster John Knox, 1995.

———. *God's Human Speech: A Practical Theology of Proclamation*. Grand Rapids: Eerdmans, 1997.

Belenky, Mary Field, et al. *Women's Ways of Knowing: The Development of Self, Voice, and Mind*. New York: Basic, 1986.

Best, Wallace D. *Passionately Human, No Less Divine*. Princeton: Princeton University Press, 2005.

Birke, Lynda. *Feminism and the Biological Body*. Brunswick, NJ: Rutgers University Press, 2000.

Bordo, Susan. *Unbearable Weight: Feminism, Western Culture, and the Body*. Berkeley: University of California Press, 2003.

Bozarth-Campbell, Alla. *The Word's Body: An Incarnational Aesthetic of Communication*. Tuscaloosa: University of Alabama Press, 1979.

Brekus, Catherine. *Strangers and Pilgrims: Female Preaching in America, 1740–1845*. Chapel Hill: University of North Carolina Press, 1998.

Brenneman, Laura L. "Embodiment in Paul: Making Christ Visible." *Vision* 17 (2016) 6–14.

Brenon, Anne. "The Voice of the Good Woman: An Essay on the Pastoral and Sacerdotal Role of Women in the Cathar Church." In Kienzle and Walker, *Women Preachers and Prophets*, 114–33.

Broadus, John. *A Treatise on the Preparation and Delivery of Sermons*. New York: Armstrong, 1898.

Busch, Thomas. "Existentialism: The 'New Philosophy.'" In *Merleau-Ponty: Key Concepts*, edited by Rosalyn Diprose and Jack Reynolds, 30–43. New York: Routledge, 2014.

Butler, Judith. *Excitable Speech: A Politics of the Performative*. New York: Routledge, 1997.

———. *Gender Trouble: Feminism and the Subversion of Identity*. New York: Routledge, 1990.

———. *The Psychic Life of Power: Theories of Subjection*. Stanford: Stanford University Press, 1997.

Childers, Jana. *Performing the Word: Preaching as Theatre*. Nashville: Abingdon, 1998.

———. "The Preacher's Body." *Princeton Seminary Bulletin* 27 (2006) 222–37.

Chrysostomos, Archimandrite. *Orthodox Liturgical Dress: An Historical Treatment*. Brookline, MA: Holy Cross Orthodox Press, 1981.

Collier-Thomas, Bettye. *Daughters of Thunder: Black Women Preachers and Their Sermons, 1850–1979*. San Francisco: Jossey-Bass, 1998.

Cruickshank, William M., ed. *Cerebral Palsy: A Developmental Disability*. 3rd ed. Syracuse: Syracuse University Press, 1976.

Dana, Joseph. *A New American Selection of Lessons in Reading and Speaking*. Boston: Samuel Hall, 1792.

Down, Martin. "The Costume of the Clergy." *Theology* 85 (1982) 346–53.

Edwards, O. C., Jr. *A History of Preaching*. Nashville: Abingdon, 2004.

Farley, Todd. "The Use of the Body in the Performance of Proclamation." In *Performance in Preaching: Bringing the Sermon to Life*, edited by Jana Childers and Clayton J. Schmit, 117–38. Grand Rapids: Baker Academic, 2008.

Fischer-Mirkin, Toby. *Dress Code: Understanding the Hidden Meanings of Women's Clothes*. New York: Clarkson Potter, 1995.

Flinders, Carol Lee. *Enduring Grace: Living Portraits of Seven Women Mystics*. New York: HarperCollins, 1993.

Florence, Anna Carter. *Preaching as Testimony*. Louisville: Westminster John Knox, 2007.

Fortunati, Vita, et al., eds, *The Controversial Women's Body*. Bologna: Bononia University Press, 2003.

Frank, Arthur. "Bringing Bodies Back In: A Decade in Review." *Theory, Culture and Society* 7 (1990) 131–62.

———. *The Wounded Storyteller: Body, Illness, and Ethics*. Chicago: University of Chicago Press, 1995.

Fuss, Diane. *Essentially Speaking: Feminism, Nature, and Difference*. New York: Routledge, 1989.

Gadow, Sally. "Body and Self: A Dialectic." *Journal of Medicine and Philosophy* 5 (1980) 172–85.

Gilligan, Carol. *In a Different Voice: Psychological Theory and Women's Development*. Cambridge: Harvard University Press, 1982.

Green, Roger J. *Catherine Booth: A Biography of the Cofounder of the Salvation Army*. Grand Rapids: Baker, 1996.

Griffith, R. Marie. *Born Again Bodies: Flesh and Spirit in American Christianity*. Los Angeles: University of California Press, 2004.

Grimshaw, Jean. "Working Out with Merleau-Ponty." In *Women's Bodies: Discipline and Transgression*, edited by Jane Arthurs and Jean Grimshaw, 91–116. New York: Cassell, 1999.

Grosz, Elizabeth. *Volatile Bodies: Toward a Corporeal Feminism*. Bloomington: Indiana University Press, 1994.

Haltunen, Karen. *Confidence Men and Painted Women: A Study of Middle-Class Culture in America, 1830–1870*. New Haven: Yale University Press, 1982.

Hartman, Tracy Lee. "Feminist Norms in Preaching: Fact or Fiction? A Contextual Study of the Preaching of Baptist Women." PhD diss., Union Theological Seminary, 2001.

Hogan, Lucy Lind. "The Overthrow of the Monopoly of the Pulpit: A Longitudinal Case Study of the Cultural Conversation Advocating the Preaching and Ordination of Women in American Methodism, 1859–1924." PhD diss., University of Maryland, College Park, 1995.

Hollander, Anne. *Sex and Suits*. New York: Knopf, 1994.

Holliday, Ruth, and John Hassard, eds. *Contested Bodies*. New York, Routledge, 2001.

Hudson, Mary Linnie. "Shall Women Preach? Or the Question Answered: The Ministry of Louisa M. Woosley in the Cumberland Presbyterian Church, 1887–1942." PhD diss., Vanderbilt University, 1992.

Humez, Jean McMahon, ed. *Gifts of Power: The Writings of Rebecca Jackson, Black Visionary, Shaker Eldress*. Amherst: University of Massachusetts Press, 1981.

Jansen, Katherine Ludwig. "Maria Magdalena: Apostolorum Apostola." In Kienzle and Walker, *Women Preachers and Prophets*, 57–96.

Johnson, Luke Timothy. *The Revelatory Body: Theology as Inductive Art*. Grand Rapids: Eerdmans, 2015.

Jones, Serene. *Feminist Theory and Christian Theology: Cartographies of Grace*. Minneapolis: Fortress, 2000.

Karpf, Anne. *The Human Voice: How This Extraordinary Instrument Reveals Essential Clues about Who We Are*. New York: Bloomsbury, 2006.

Kemper, Deane A. *Effective Preaching*. Philadelphia: Westminster, 1985.

Kienzle, Beverly M. "The Prostitute-Preacher: Patterns of Polemic against Medieval Waldensians Women Preachers." In Kienzle and Walker, *Women Preachers and Prophets*, 99–113.

Kienzle, Beverly M., and Pamela J. Walker, eds. *Women Preachers and Prophets through Two Millennia of Christianity*. Berkeley: University of California Press, 1998.

Kim, Eunjoo Mary. "Conversational Learning: A Feminist Pedagogy for Teaching Preaching." *Theology and Religion* 5 (2002) 169–77.

———. *Women Preaching: Theology and Practice through the Ages*. Cleveland: Pilgrim, 2004.

King, Karen. "Prophetic Power and Women's Authority: The Case of the Gospel of Mary (Magdalene)." In Kienzle and Walker, *Women Preachers and Prophets*, 21–41.

Kirby, Vicki. *Judith Butler: Live Theory*. London: Continuum, 2006.

Larson, Rebecca. *Daughters of Light: Quaker Women Preaching and Prophesying in the Colonies and Abroad, 1700–1775*. New York: Knopf, 1999.

Lawless, Elaine. *God's Peculiar People: Women's Voices and Folk Tradition in a Pentecostal Church*. Lexington: University Press of Kentucky, 1998.

———. *Handmaidens of the Lord*. Philadelphia: University of Pennsylvania Press, 1988.

———. *Holy Women, Wholly Women: Sharing Ministries of Wholeness through Life Stories and Reciprocal Ethnography*. Philadelphia: University of Pennsylvania Press, 1993.

———. "The Issue of Blood—Reinstating Women into the Tradition." In Kienzle and Walker, *Women Preachers and Prophets*, 1–20.

Leder, Drew. *The Absent Body*. Chicago: University of Chicago Press, 1990.

Lindman, Janet M., and Michele L. Tarter, eds. *A Centre of Wonders: The Body in Early America*. Ithaca: Cornell University Press, 2001.

Long, Thomas G. *The Witness of Preaching*. 2nd ed. Louisville: Westminster John Knox, 2005.

Longhurst, Robyn. *Maternities: Gender, Bodies, and Space*. New York: Routledge, 2008.

Macalister, R. A. S. *Ecclesiastical Vestments: Their Development and History*. London: Stock, 1896.

Mahmood, Saba. "Agency, Performativity, and the Feminist Subject." In *Bodily Citations: Religion and Judith Butler*, edited by Ellen T. Armour and Susan M. St. Ville, 177–221. New York: Columbia University Press, 2006.

Mayo, Janet. *A History of Ecclesiastical Dress*. London: Batsford, 1984.

McClure, John S. *The Four Codes of Preaching: Rhetorical Strategies*. Westminster John Knox, 2003.

————, et al. *Listening to Listeners: Homiletical Case Studies*. St. Louis: Chalice, 2004.

McGee, Lee. *Wrestling with the Patriarchs*. Nashville: Abingdon, 1996.

McKenzie, Alyce M. "At the Intersection of Actio Divina and Homo Performans: Embodiment and Evocation." In *Performance in Preaching: Bringing the Sermon to Life*, edited by Jana Childers and Clayton J. Schmit, 53–66. Grand Rapids: Baker Academic, 2008.

McNeill, David. *Hand and Mind: What Gestures Reveal about Thought*. Chicago: University of Chicago Press, 1992.

Merleau-Ponty, Maurice. *Phenomenology of Perception*. Translated by Colin Smith. New York: Routledge, 1945.

Moi, Toril. *What Is a Woman? And Other Essays*. Oxford: Oxford University Press, 2001.

Mountford, Roxanne. *The Gendered Pulpit: Preaching in American Protestant Spaces*. Carbondale: Southern Illinois University Press, 2003.

Muessig, Carolyn. "Prophecy and Song: Teaching and Preaching by Medieval Women." In Kienzle and Walker, *Women Preachers and Prophets*, 146–58.

Muir, Elizabeth. *Petticoats in the Pulpit: The Story of Early 19th-Century Methodist Preachers in Upper Canada*. Toronto: United Church, 1991.

Mulligan, Mary A., et al. *Believing in Preaching: What Listeners Hear in Sermons*. St. Louis: Chalice, 2005.

Negrin, Llewellyn. *Appearance and Identity: Fashioning the Body in Postmodernity*. New York: Palgrave Macmillan, 2008.

Norén, Carol M. *The Woman in the Pulpit*. Nashville: Abingdon, 1991.

Parton, Christine E. "Voice." In *The Concise Encyclopedia of Preaching*, edited by William H. Willimon and Richard Lischer, 495. Louisville: Westminster John Knox, 1995.

Rubinstein, Ruth P. *Dress Codes: Meanings and Messages in American Culture*. 2nd ed. Boulder, CO: Westview, 2001.

Rusconi, Roberto. "Women's Sermons at the End of the Middle Ages: Texts from the Blessed and Images of the Saints." In Kienzle and Walker, *Women Preachers and Prophets*, 173–91.

Schechner, Richard. *Performance Theory*. New York: Routledge, 2003.

Sentilles, Sarah. *A Church of Her Own: What Happens When a Woman Takes the Pulpit*. New York, Harcourt, 2008.

Shuster, Marguerite. "The Truth and Truthfulness: Theological Reflections on Preaching and Performance." In *Performance in Preaching: Bringing the Sermon to Life*, edited by Jana Childers and Clayton J. Schmit, 19–36. Grand Rapids: Baker Academic, 2008.

Smith, Christine. *Weaving the Sermon: Preaching in a Feminist Perspective*. Louisville: John Knox, 1989.

Smith, Hilary Dansey. *Preaching in the Spanish Golden Age: A Study of Some Preachers in the Reign of Philip III*. Oxford: Oxford University Press, 1978.

Smith, Ted A. *The New Measures: A Theological History of Democratic Practice*. Cambridge: Cambridge University Press, 2007.

———. "A Practical History of Preaching." Unpublished manuscript. Department of Religion, Vanderbilt University.

Spurgeon, Charles Haddon. *Lectures to My Students*. Peabody: Hendrickson, 2010.

Stevenson, Karen. "Hairy Business: Organizing the Gendered Self." In *Contested Bodies*, edited by Ruth Holliday and John Hassard, 137–54. London: Routledge, 2001.

Stjerna, Krisi. "What Will They Wear?" *Seminary Ridge Review* 3 (2001) 44–46.

Sutton, Matthew Avery. *Aimee Semple McPherson and the Resurrection of Christian America*. Cambridge: Harvard University Press, 2007.

Tannen, Deborah. *You Just Don't Understand: Women and Men in Conversation*. New York: HarperCollins, 1990.

Tisdale, Nora. "Women's Ways of Communicating: A New Blessing for Preaching." In *Women, Gender and Christian Community*, edited by E. Jane Dempsey Douglass, 104–16. Louisville: Westminster John Knox, 1997.

Turner, Mary D., and Mary L. Hudson. *Saved from Silence: Finding Women's Voice in Preaching*. St. Louis: Chalice, 1999.

Turner, Victor Witter. *The Ritual Process: Structure and Anti-Structure*. New York: de Gruyter, 1995.

Walker, Pamela J. "A Chaste and Fervid Eloquence: Catherine Booth and the Ministry of Women in the Salvation Army." In Kienzle and Walker, *Women Preachers and Prophets*, 288–302.

Walters, Gwyn. "The Body in the Pulpit." In *The Preacher and Preaching: Reviving the Art in the Twentieth Century*, edited by Samuel T. Logan Jr., 445–62. Phillipsburg, NJ: Presbyterian and Reformed, 1986.

Ward, Richard F. "Performance Turns in Homiletics." *Reformed Liturgy and Music* 30 (1996). https://www.religion-online.org/blog/article/performance-turns-in-homiletics.

———. *Speaking of the Holy: The Art of Communication in Preaching*. St. Louis: Chalice, 2001.

Weber, Sandra, and Claudia Mitchell, eds. *Not Just Any Dress: Narratives of Memory, Body, and Identity*. New York: Lang, 2004.

Webster, Noah. *An American Selection of Lessons in Reading and Speaking*. Philadelphia: Young and M'Culloch, 1787.

Weinstein, Victoria [pseud., PeaceBang]. "Your Preachin' and Pastorin' Paws." *Beauty Tips for Ministers* (blog), November 2007. http://beautytipsforministers.com/2007/11/05/your-preachin-and-pastorin-paws/.

Weiss, Gail Weiss, ed. *Intertwinings: Interdisciplinary Encounters with Merleau-Ponty*. Albany: State University of New York Press, 2008.

Weitz, Rose. *Rapunzel's Daughters: What Women's Hair Tells Us about Women's Lives*. New York: Farrar, Straus and Giroux, 2004.

Westfall, Rachel. "The Pregnant/Birthing Body: Negotiations of Personal Autonomy." In *Gender, Identity and Place: Understanding Feminist Geographies*, edited by Linda McDowell, 263–76. Minneapolis: University of Minnesota Press, 1999.

Williams, Rowan. *Why Study the Past? The Quest for the Historical Church*. Grand Rapids: Eerdmans, 2005.

Wilson, Tamsin. "Temporality, Materiality: Towards a Body in Time." In *Women's Bodies: Discipline and Transgression*, edited by Jane Arthurs and Jean Grimshaw, 48–66. New York: Cassell, 1999.

Young, Iris Marion. "Lived Body versus Gender: Reflections on Social Structure and Subjectivity." In *On Female Body Experience: "Throwing Like a Girl" and Other Essays*, 12–26. Oxford: Oxford University Press, 2005.

———."Pregnant Embodiment." In *On Female Body Experience: "Throwing Like a Girl" and Other Essays*, 46–61. Oxford: Oxford University Press, 2005.

———."Throwing like a Girl: A Phenomenology of Feminine Body Comportment, Motility, and Spatiality." In *On Female Body Experience: "Throwing Like a Girl" and Other Essays*, 27–45. Oxford: Oxford University Press, 2005.

Ziel, Catherine A. "Mother Tongue / Father Tongue: Gender-Linked Differences in Language Use and Their Influence on the Perceived Authority of the Preacher." PhD diss., Princeton Theological Seminary, 1991.

Zink-Sawyer, Beverly. *From Preachers to Suffragists: Woman's Rights and Religious Convictions in the Lives of Three Nineteenth-Century American Clergywomen*. Louisville: Westminster John Knox, 2003.

CPSIA information can be obtained
at www.ICGtesting.com
Printed in the USA
FSHW011942141218
54498FS